OVERLOOKED

BRIDGETTE CAMERON RIDENOUR

WITH
RENE GUTTERIDGE

Overlooked

© Copyright 2023 by Bridgette Cameron Ridenour

With Rene Gutteridge

Edited and published by Writing Momentum LLC

Cover design, print and ebook formatting by Writing Momentum LLC

PRAISE FOR OVERLOOKED

When we four were kids, if you had asked me who in our family was the biggest entertainer, most talented dancer, and biggest drama queen, I would have told you, "Bridgette!" She's one year younger than me (although for one month of the year, she argues we are the same age), but sings, dances, and speaks with the youthful spunk and enthusiasm of someone half her age! Bridgette is fun-sized, funny, and fierce. In her new book, *Overlooked*, she will tug at your heart, make you roar with laughter, and lead you to the One who loves you best.

Kirk Cameron
Actor, Producer

Bridgette is the friend everyone wants in their corner, the dance partner you would want through life. You have always been the life of every party and you keep me laughing until I'm utterly crying. The way I have always seen you, as your younger sister, is no different in how I see you now. I thank God He made you mine.

Melissa Fleming
Child of God, Sister, Wife/Mom Extraordinaire

Bridgette will always be my little big sister, with a bubbly personality and dance moves that steal the show! Forever patient (hello... riding as a passenger to me driving her car at 15 with my permit to the studio and back!), always fun, and a great teammate. Today, Bridgette is a mama bear, protective to her core when it comes to family and friends, a fighter for what's just and right especially when it comes straight from her gut. I've learned a lot from my little big sister over the years and I'm forever grateful to God to be yours.

Candace Cameron Bure
Actress, Producer, CEO CandyRock Entertainment

Encouraging and inspiring, Bridgette Cameron Ridenour's new book sparks laughter and evokes tears. It's authentic, unflinching, and its lessons can be applied in your life starting today. Settle into a comfortable chair and let Bridgette take you on a spiritual journey that will open your eyes and fill your heart.

Lee Strobel
New York Times Best-selling Author

Bridgette was a surprise guest at our most recent fundraising event, featuring her brother, Kirk Cameron. Bridgette communicated with boldness and passion, and everyone in the room clearly felt her emotion. She moved our audience with her story...and I can see Bridgette moving audiences of all ages to action, spreading a message of Hope wherever she goes.

Heather Lawless
CEO and Founder, Reliance Center

Bridgette's testimony is a God-given story that will impact the lives of those who are searching for the real meaning of purpose in their life.

Todd Dunn
Lead Pastor, 2nd Mile Church

Bridgette is a blessing. God blesses so many but very few are like her. She asked, "God, why did you choose our family?" Because He knew none of you would be silent in sharing His goodness to the world.

Judy Sessions Belshee-Toernblom
Casting Agent / Director

Hearing Bridgette's testimony had me in tears, both of sorrow and mostly joy. Her testimony will give so many people the faith and hope they are lacking.

Ryley Rose Bausmith

Summer in the Psalms Women's Conference Attendee

Bridgette is a remarkable woman with a one-of-a-kind story that is for all ages. Her passion through every stage of her life will have you crying, laughing, and rejoicing, reminding us to always lean towards Jeremiah 29:11.

Hope Burke

Executive Director, Helping Hand of Hope

Bridgette Cameron Ridenour has a way of pulling you into her story, making it feel as though you walked beside her as she fought to understand why her God-given talents were being overlooked by an entire industry. Bridgette vulnerably shares about the struggles she faced emotionally and spiritually, allowing us to explore our own vulnerability. Bridgette brings light to the stage of God's world and shines brightly for His purpose.

Jennifer Osler-Bolton

Host of The Lavender Dahlia Podcast

Lord, I dedicate this book to you.

Thank you for writing my story better than I ever could have.

I lay this book at your feet and pray it will bring Honor and Glory to Your Kingdom. Amen.

CONTENTS

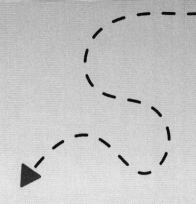

PROLOGUE

May 27, 2015

IT SEEMED ALL SOUND HAD VANISHED from the world. My ears rang with nothing but terror. My attention snapped to the front windshield. A man slid across the hood of our car.

"Get out! Get out!" the man yelled. "Get out of the car! Fire!"

The kids' screams began. It was hard to hear what else he was saying, but his expression said it all. This was life-or-death.

John pointed to my door. The smoke was choking now, and I could barely see anything.

I grabbed for the handle, and it opened. I quickly whisked the kids out, but we were engulfed in black smoke and a cloak of dirt that wouldn't leave us.

"Over here!"

The voice was faint. Unfamiliar.

"Over here!"

We turned but didn't know to what or whom.

"Over here, this way!"

I gathered the kids. We could barely see each other through the fog of dust and smoke.

Their eyes were so round, so scared. I tried to steady my next words and make them count. They needed to hear this and obey it, without question. I looked at each of them for no more than a half-second.

"Run..."

It almost sounded like a whisper. *Run to the voice.*

They turned, and off they ran, into the unknown, vanishing right in front of me.

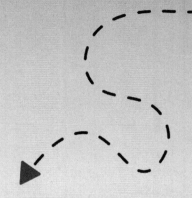

CHAPTER 1
A FEW GROWING PAINS

I WAS BORN in Panorama City and raised in San Fernando Valley, one of the strangest regions in California. It's a hard place to understand if you don't live there.

Small rolling hills separate two parts of the valley: the rich part and the poor part. We weren't by any means poor, but compared to the other side of the hills, where all the movie stars lived, we were penniless. More aptly put, we were middle-class.

My dad was a middle school math and PE teacher. My mom was a stay-at-home mom to us four kids and taught macrame classes in our garage. My brother, Kirk, was the oldest. I came next, then Melissa, and Candace was the youngest.

We were all happy and well-adjusted kids, but I was probably the happiest. I was a naturally eternal optimist, though I hadn't any idea at that age what that was. And I couldn't have been more of a Valley Girl. I simply loved all the things of my era: neon clothes, big, teased hair, the verbiage, which I used with great enthusiasm, and the music. There was nothing I loved more than dancing in my room to everything from the Go-Gos to Janet Jackson.

My sisters and I shared a room down the hall from Kirk. We spent our free time playing with our Strawberry Shortcake and Cabbage Patch dolls, making up dance routines for them. We couldn't pass up a chance to use our Donnie and Marie microphones to entertain our long-suffering parents. They were always eager to hear us, though I'm certain they were exhausted at the end of the day.

The three of us made up our own secret language. Boy did that come in handy, especially when we were planning our revenge on Kirk, who constantly entertained himself by teasing and tormenting us in one particular way: sitting on us, pinning our arms down, and letting spit slowly stretch down from his mouth to our faces.

I'd scream and turn my head from side to side, hoping not to be touched by the long, gross strand of spit. Then, with one quick inhale back, Kirk would draw the drool back into his mouth. Not a drop would touch our faces. He always stepped right up to the line of what would get him in trouble.

Because there were four kids, and they wanted to keep a good eye on us, Mom and Dad always let our house be a safe place for other kids. Everyone was welcome. No one had to ask to come over. Friends and family gathered at our house for everything from birthdays to graduations to pre-prom. You name it, it was probably at our house. I've often said, if those walls could talk, boy the stories that they would tell!

Even before we entered the Hollywood scene, life was magical. Every Sunday, our entire family—aunts, uncles, cousins, friends, grandparents—would meet at Zuma beach, specifically Lifeguard Tower 12.

Off the famed Pacific Coast Highway in Malibu, Zuma Beach is popular with both surfers and families alike. It also has 14 lifeguard towers.

We always gathered at Tower 12, which was encouraged by the fire department, who patrolled the beaches. Swimmers were instructed to avoid the waters between towers 8 and 9, where rip currents were particularly prevalent. But back then, we weren't thinking much about safety. My siblings and I were mostly thinking about fun and food.

The day started early for beach prepping. We formed a line at the kitchen counter, where everybody built sandwiches, gathered fruit and vegetables, or put everything in baggies. Some of us had the duty of packing the car that morning. Those who didn't had the not-so-great duty of unpacking the car at the end of the day.

Once there, we spent the day boogie boarding, body surfing, and building pyramid towers. We loved hanging out with each other...and of course getting into some mischief too.

Sometimes, the four of us rummaged through the other coolers for cookies, chips, and Capri Suns. My parents were the health-conscious type, and sometimes those alfalfa sprout sandwiches just got to be too much.

The sunsets at Zuma beach couldn't have been more beautiful, and often we'd settle ourselves down, a difficult thing to do, to soak them in. After a day of hard play, it was always nice to just sit and watch.

Then it was time to pack up and head back home, but we never forgot to stop at the local Foster Freeze for our chocolate-dipped ice cream cones. This was how we assumed we would always spend Sundays—together, at the ocean.

Between beach trips, family vacations, and sibling squabbles,

I occasionally found myself in my room alone. That was the place I dreamed of performing. I loved to dance, sing, and act. I twirled across my room, dreaming of playing this role or that, being a big singer or dancing in some Broadway show.

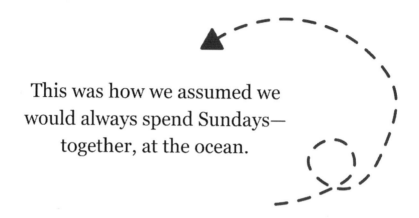

This was how we assumed we would always spend Sundays— together, at the ocean.

It was during this time, when we lived in the apartment in Northridge, that we met the Rich family. Adam Rich was our age, and one of our favorite playmates. Adam was a child actor and had already landed two movies when we met him.

My mom and Adam's mom, Fran, became good friends and it was nice to have another family that our parents could trust. Fran often talked to my mom about getting us kids into acting, but my mom wasn't interested. She didn't think it was a good idea, and school was ultra-important to our family.

Soon, Adam became successful enough that they relocated from Northridge to Hollywood. He'd just landed a role on a TV show called *Eight is Enough*. With that, our playmate of two years, and my mom's friend, were gone to the other side of the hill.

One day, my mom and Fran reconnected at a grocery store.

They caught up as moms do, and my mom showed Fran a current picture of the four of us.

"Oh, Barb!" Fran said. "You MUST get the kids into acting. I know an agent. I can connect you with her. Really, they're just so adorable. You must!"

Mom wasn't too sure. We didn't have an entertainment background at all.

"Just let me take a picture to the agent and show her. She can say yes or no. If she says no, I promise not to bring it up again."

"Well," Mom said, "if any of our kids would be interested, it'd be Bridgette. All day long that girl is singing and dancing, wearing out the Donnie and Marie microphone we got her!"

They laughed and continued catching up.

Mom came home and thought about it. Yes, all four of us were adorable, but this seemed right up my alley.

She talked it over with my dad, and they decided it might be a fun activity for all of us, something, perhaps, to keep us "out of trouble," earn some extra money, and even develop a new skill set.

A few days later, Mom got a call. The agent wanted to see us!

No one was more excited about this opportunity than me.

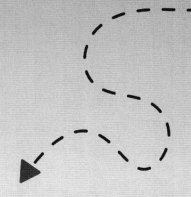

CHAPTER 2
IRIS SAID "NO" TODAY

THE DAY CAME for our auditions. We all piled into the VW van and drove to downtown L.A. My dad pulled to the curb, and we tumbled out, we girls hyped up on nerves and excitement. Mom scrambled to get all the sock rollers out of Melissa's and my hair. I stood on the sidewalk underneath a towering skyscraper that housed the agent's office. I felt small but mighty against its shadow. My excitement for the day couldn't be contained. My brother was the least enthusiastic about it all, but I could tell even he was at least curious about what was going to happen.

As Dad drove off, Mom took the four of us, including little Candace, through the glass doors. The lobby was expansive but unadorned. As we rode the elevator, my heart pounded in my chest—not out of nervousness, but excitement.

I exited the elevator and spotted two enormous oak doors at the end of a long hallway—at least it seemed long to my 8-year-old self. On the door read a placard: *The Iris Burton Agency*. By the time the Cameron clan arrived on this sunny afternoon, Iris

Burton was already a well-known and very successful Holly-wood agent. In the early part of her career, she'd been a dancer on Broadway. She had moved to Hollywood and danced in films too, including *Top Banana.* Her showgirl brass served her well as she went on to become a rare specimen—a successful female Hollywood power agent. She worked for an agency at first, then started her own in 1977.

Iris specialized in representing children, and she couldn't have had a better eye for talent. At one point, it was said that she had a client in every child sitcom on television. As one *New York Times* article put it, she was known for "plucking kids out of obscurity."

We were certainly obscure. We couldn't have been more unaware of what we were walking into, honestly. This just seemed like a fun thing to do—something to keep us busy. Little did we know it was about to change all our lives.

Inside her office, the first thing I noticed was the large photo-covered wall of child stars she represented. I couldn't believe how many I recognized from their work: River Phoenix and his siblings; C. Thomas Howell; Henry Thomas; Drew Barrymore; Mary Kate and Ashley Olsen; Tori Spelling; Fred Savage; Jerry O'Connell; Corey Feldman; Hilary and Hailey Duff; Kirsten Dunst; Jaleel White... to name a few.

This wall of faces seemed to blur together into one notion: *I'm here to make you famous.*

Iris greeted us right away, saying hello in her signature deep, raspy voice, her New York accent thick and pronounced. Curly brown hair framed pretty features, and she held a long cigarette between her pointer and middle fingers, showcased by exquisite fingernails. She seemed iconic in every sense of the word.

She brought us into her office. She sat down in an intimidating leather chair behind a large oak desk that was piled with papers and scripts. Behind her, another wall of kids' headshots loomed. Everything about the place screamed success. If you were with Iris, you were the cream of the crop.

My mother introduced herself with a polite hand. "Hi Mrs. Burton, I'm Barbara Cameron."

"Call me Iris," she said. "Have a seat." It was right to business. "I'm going to give your kids some commercial sides to look over. Once they've looked over them, we're going to put them in front of the camera and have them read it." She handed my mom the sides. "You don't have to memorize them."

She gave us a few more instructions. I noticed right away that Iris talked to us like adults. She wasn't pulling punches. She made it clear—this was business. If we were to be her clients, we were going to work hard for her and take it seriously. This, perhaps, was what made her successful, what made her talented kids rise to the top. They stopped thinking of themselves as kids and got serious about their careers in the entertainment business.

I sat up straighter and glanced at Kirk, who was swinging his legs and picking at something on his shirt. My sense of excitement was now met with a hint of nervousness. It wouldn't be the last time I felt that mix. Later, I discovered that Iris had a unique way of turning this professional prowess on and off. Inside these walls of entertainment, it was all business: whatever you do, *don't disappoint her*. Outside the walls of entertainment, though, she was kind and motherly. Her love language was gift giving—lots of it. She really loved kids.

But for now, at this initial meeting, she was an intimidating, expressionless woman. She watched each of us carefully, that glamorous cigarette dangling from her fingers, and scrutiny oozing from her eyes. Not in a judgmental way, but in a way that could spot the "it" factor, even before a kid knew how to try to have it or even what it was.

After a little bit, she instructed us to go into another room—the audition room. Mom was flustered, trying to manage Candace and the three of us as we asked questions and struggled to know what to do. Kirk, however, seemed unaffected by it all.

"Say your name first," Iris rasped. "And tell me your age. Then read your piece."

Kirk was up first. His piece went something like, "Hey Mom! I'm the strongest man in the world!" I think it was for He-Man. Then he also read for McDonald's. "Hey, Mom! Let's go to McDonald's!"

Melissa and I were next, performing auditions for Barbie and McDonald's. Candace then danced and sang, being her cute four-year-old self.

After we auditioned, we sat outside while Iris brought Mom back into her office. Kirk got picked right away. "He just has a look I like," Iris told Mom. She wanted Melissa too. Candace was too young at four, but Iris said to bring her back when she was six, the youngest age that she would take a child actor.

Mom leaned forward. "What about Bridgette? You're not taking Bridgette? Out of all my kids, Bridgette's the one who really wants to do this."

"She needs braces," Iris declared, circling her hand around her own mouth. "The teeth, you know. Crooked." Iris seemed not to have a twinge of sympathy about it. "Bring her back when the braces are off."

As a mother now, I imagine my mom walking out of the

office to find us, trying to figure out how to break the news to me. A mother's heart hurts so easily for their kids. How many breaths did she have to take before turning into the room where we waited? She must've dragged her feet to buy herself time, searching for the best words to try to explain it, if there even was a "best."

She took me aside gently, her eyes soft and trying to hide her hurt for me. "Bridgette, honey, Iris said 'no' today."

She explained the braces. My little mind tried to comprehend it all. What was so wrong with braces? Why can't kids with braces be on TV? While the rest of my siblings were blessed with straight teeth and aligned jaws, I hit the lottery with problems in both areas. Our dentist had already informed my parents I would need lots of work.

The disappointment that day ran deep, but I managed to keep a positive attitude—something of a rare gift that I was born with, as some testing would later show. Mom said I just needed to be patient. My time would come. So, I kept singing, dancing, and putting on little plays for the neighborhood. I had dreams—big dreams—and crooked teeth weren't going to stop them.

I'd get the occasional audition request when they wanted a kid with braces, but even then, I kept getting the equivalent of what I'd heard the very first time: "Iris said 'no' today."

In the meantime, I watched my brother's acting career take off. He was an overnight hit, winning at everything he did. He hardly seemed capable of failing, but he wasn't that impressed with any of it. In fact, while I waited in the wings for any small chance, he fought my mom tooth and nail about going to auditions since that meant he sometimes missed recess or P.E., activities he was much more interested in.

When he auditioned for *Growing Pains*, he and Mom were running very late. They were stuck on the 405 freeway, thanks in part to Kirk arguing about going when she came to pick him up. Mom was upset. This was a big audition for him, and Iris took these things seriously. Kirk was still fuming about missing P.E. Everything was going wrong and about to get worse.

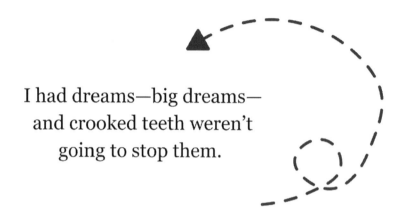

I had dreams—big dreams—
and crooked teeth weren't
going to stop them.

Mom dropped Kirk off on the lot and he scurried inside, searching for the casting office. When he finally found it, only one person remained, the camera guy, who was packing up his equipment.

"I'm here to audition for some pilot. *Growing Pains*, I think, is the name."

"Sorry kid," the cameraman said, zipping up his bag, "you missed it. Everyone's gone. Auditions are over."

"No, no, no, no, no..." Kirk went into a sheer panic. "Everyone's going to be mad at me," he said. "My mom. Iris." He swallowed. "Iris," he repeated. He stepped into the room and pleaded. "Please let me just tape this so they're not mad at me."

The camera guy sighed. "Okay." He set everything back up—

which shows the kind of magnetism Kirk already had, the "star power," if you will. What overly worked camera guy could otherwise be convinced to reset a camera for a teen actor who was afraid of getting in trouble with his mom and agent?

The rest is history for Kirk.

Meanwhile, I was still struggling with crooked teeth and an underbite.

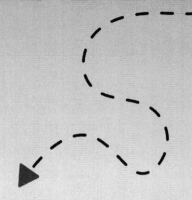

CHAPTER 3
LIGHTS, CAMERA, HOLLYWOOD

BEFORE ALL THE Hollywood parties arrived in our lives, our family celebrated Kirk's success in our living room in front of the TV. By now we'd moved closer to Hollywood, to a four-bedroom ranch-style home in Canoga Park (now called West Hills), on Sausalito Avenue in the San Fernando Valley of Los Angeles. He was landing commercial after commercial, everything from He-Man to 409. Friends of ours called our house phone to let us know they'd seen one of his commercials. We'd scramble to the TV, find the station, and wait for it to run again.

One commercial holds an interesting memory for me. Kirk was scheduled to film a Kool-Aid commercial. He and I, being the oldest, spent a lot of time riding around on Big Wheels. California has a hilly landscape, and there was never a place that didn't have a hill begging to be ridden like the wind. As luck would have it, our neighborhood had one of the best ones.

On this particular day, Kirk had an idea—well, the original one anyway—and it seemed amazing at the time. I had an idea for a slight modification, and that turned out differently than either of us imagined it going in our heads.

Kirk proposed that I pull him on my Big Wheel while he rode his skateboard behind me. It seemed revolutionary in the moment, though looking back, it probably happened on every street in the neighborhood.

Being the younger and pretty adventurous little sister, I wholeheartedly agreed to the plan. We found a rope and were soon whizzing down the hill. I peddled like a fiend, and Kirk glided gracefully back and forth behind me on his skateboard.

Now, this story would probably have a less eventful ending had a little devil not popped onto my shoulder and given me an idea. As we shot down the hill, I spotted ahead of me a makeshift ramp we used for our Big Wheels. I started heading for it. Fast. I congratulated myself on how clever and hilarious I was. It worked. Kirk yelled at me from behind, waving me off, screaming like the three little sisters he'd been teasing and pranking for years.

"Bridgette! Don't go off the ramp!"

I, of course, being more mature than him, had no real intention of flying off that ramp. At the very last minute, I jerked the Big Wheel left to avoid it. I just wanted to give him a little scare.

But, you know, I was a kid. I didn't factor in, well...physics.

I also didn't factor in that Kirk wouldn't just let go of the rope.

He flew off the ramp, tumbled on the other side, and lay in the street, crying and holding his arm. I ran to get Mom and Dad. We loaded Kirk into the back of one of those long station wagons everyone had, the minivan of the day, and took him to the hospital. All I heard Kirk saying was, "Mom, am I gonna die?" over and over.

His first dramatic role. He nailed it.

I was convinced I'd killed my brother, though, which was not the plan.

He lived—thankfully.

But on the set of the Kool-Aid commercial shortly thereafter, the entire thing had to be modified to accommodate his cast.

Oops.

Soon after Kirk's commercials, Candace, a few years older now, auditioned and began landing roles too. It seemed my siblings were on the TV all the time, and despite the constant "Iris said 'no' today" swirling around my life, we had a ton of fun watching them.

It was once Kirk landed the role of *Growing Pains* that things started to get surreal.

One incident really brought it home for me. I was in our home and heard voices near the front door. I assumed Melissa had friends over. Our house was still the place everyone gathered.

I came to investigate and found a gaggle of girls, giggling and half-hysterical, cupping their hands over their mouths. They bobbed up and down with tiny half-jumps of awe.

I didn't have a clue who they were.

"What are you doing?" I asked. They didn't seem scary. They looked like they were about to cry.

"We wanted to see Kirk!" one of them squealed.

"The cleaning lady let us in the house," another explained.

I quickly ushered them out. Our cleaning lady, immersed in her own family and life, hadn't quite noticed Kirk's fame. In her defense, we had teen friends coming and going all the time. "We want to see Kirk" didn't seem out of the ordinary.

I guess I hadn't quite realized the scope of his fame yet either. I certainly hadn't expected a group of teen girls we didn't know to come into our house to see him.

As Kirk's fame climbed, it became harder and harder to ignore. Trips to amusement parks were nearly impossible, even with Kirk in disguise. I'd watch from the sidelines when Kirk made public appearances. Girls would go absolutely nuts. Screaming. Crying. "Acting 'a fool" as some might put it. All for my brother? Did they know he regularly pretended to drool on his sisters?

Candace was growing more famous too, but the truth was, we never felt like a celebrity family. My dad was still a math teacher. Mom still did macrame out of the garage. Eventually, a gate went up around our house, for security reasons. But we still fit right into the neighborhood.

Perhaps that was the naivete of it all. We were a wholesome, tight, loving family. Kirk was still the same typical teen he was when this all started, not an A-List celebrity living the Holly-wood lifestyle. Even so, we weren't left unscathed by the dark side of the industry, as we were about to find out in the scariest of ways. But even more, we would eventually find out how much God's hand of protection was around our family, all before we even knew Him.

KIRK ROSE through the ranks of fame during the golden age of TV sitcoms and young, hip, beautiful actors and actresses. The wall of kids that Iris had looming in her office grew into the faces of Hollywood—famous, successful people, all invited to the Who's-Who of celebrity parties.

Kirk was nominated over the years for several People's Choice awards. Those were always the best. Mom would take us girls shopping for dresses. We'd do our hair while Kirk had people helping him. Then we'd all pile into the very out-of-place limousine that pulled up to our typical suburban house in our typical suburban neighborhood. Unlike now, limos back then meant you were famous. The neighbors enjoyed watching our family pile in. Then we'd hit the road. As we drove by, people would gawk from their cars. There was never a doubt—whoever was riding behind those tinted windows was a "somebody." Little did they know how average our family was. We were as awed by it all as everybody else.

I was having as much fun as anyone, never thinking how sad it was that it wasn't me in the spotlight. It was fun for all of us, thanks to my parents. And the paparazzi enjoyed taking pictures of the whole family. We knew the routine well: Pose for pictures as a family, then step aside so Kirk and/or Candace could have their picture taken solo. It was what we did.

When we unloaded from the limo, Iris Burton, glamorous and confident as usual, often greeted us and posed for pictures with us. She hovered protectively like a mother hen. Flashbulbs went off everywhere, and she guided us here and there, making sure Kirk shook hands with all the right people.

While Kirk was in the prime of young Hollywood, old Hollywood was still alive and well. These two generational arms of fame often met at parties. Old Hollywood was like a dream for me. I knew all the famous actors from that era. Kirk, on the other hand, didn't have a clue who they were, so I constantly trailed behind him and said things like, "That's Bob Hope. Lucille Ball. That's Cary Grant."

Didn't he understand these were legends? I couldn't believe

it, the people I was meeting: Patty Duke. Phyllis Diller. George Burns. Betty White. Hollywood elite!

One time we were at a table with Jimmy Stewart, and Kirk leaned over for help placing his name. "Kirk!" I whispered harshly. "It's Jimmy Stewart. *Jimmy Stewart.* You can't be at a table with people like Jimmy Stewart and not know who he is!" Kirk shrugged, unaffected as usual, as I cast a starry gaze across the table.

Kirk just never could connect the face with the names. But I was more than happy to assist. Those were my favorite parties. There were also the other Hollywood parties, the Who's-Who of young Hollywood attending—Corey Feldman, Corey Haim, Alyssa Milano, River Phoenix, Adam Rich, Alfonso Ribeiro, to name a few. At those parties, our family seemed out of place most of the time, though there were a few in that crowd who didn't love the scene either. We'd somehow find each other at the back of the house or the top of the stairs and hang out quietly, getting to know one another.

One event that stands out to me is the *BOP* magazine party. They were throwing a huge party for New Kids on the Block and just we girls were invited. Mom and Dad were understand-ably leery about that kind of party. New Kids on the Block was one of the first boy bands, and there was no doubt things could get out of control. But we begged and begged and finally managed to talk them into letting our nanny, Sara, take us. Sara was also our tutor and accompanied us on set.

However, once we got there, we realized it was going to be the kind of party where actors and actresses moved in groups, formed cliques, and decided to prove to each other who was "better."

There were shallow, "Oh, hi! How are you?" greetings, and whispers of drugs and alcohol being offered in dark spaces.

It was not our scene—not by a long shot. We mostly went to parties where adults attended, so we were clearly out of place. It showed.

Sara, Melissa, Candace, and I somehow found a quiet place off to the side near some grand staircase. We sat and just watched people. Nobody seemed to notice us until the star brothers in New Kids on the Block, Jonathan and Jordan Knight, came over and politely introduced themselves.

We chatted with them for a while, and they were refreshingly down-to-earth. Donnie Wahlberg soon came over and joined in. It was easygoing and genuine, like normal teens hanging out and getting to know each other.

One of them eventually said, "These kinds of parties are not really our thing," which we all found funny since the whole party was thrown in their honor.

Then one of them said, "Really, the whole reason we were excited to come is because we heard the Cameron girls were going to be here."

"Yeah," another said, "we were just super excited to meet you all."

That started a years-long friendship with the guys in the group. We'd go to their concerts when they were nearby and go backstage to say hello and catch up. I developed a crush on Jonathan. Candace liked Joey McIntyre. Melissa liked Donnie. Donnie had fun "proposing" marriage to Melissa one night at a party.

We lost touch with them for a while in our adulthood. When they came into town for their comeback tour, we decided to go see them. Backstage, we stood off to the side and waited.

Candace's publicist went over to Jonathan and pointed toward us. He blinked, confused, then narrowed his eyes at me. Suddenly a lightbulb went off. He remembered us! We had a great time catching up.

Though I hadn't landed any big acting roles like I'd hoped, I was still living a kind of Hollywood dream. I was determined to soak it all up.

But the dream of all dreams came true with celebrity encounters the day I met Paula Abdul on the set of *Full House*. I was standing in for Andrea Barber. Paula was dating John Stamos at the time, and choreographing for Janet Jackson, which was my dream job. John Stamos, being the kind soul that he is, knew how much I loved her and made sure I got to meet her that day. Perfectly exquisite, she talked with me for a while. I was over the moon.

A couple of years later, while we were walking the red carpet for some event, we heard John Stamos was arriving with Paula. We lingered and waited for them to get out of the limo. Candace greeted John, and Paula, unbelievably, spotted me and approached. We chatted like we were old friends. I couldn't believe it! It was one of the best nights ever.

But against the flash of the bulbs and glint of the tinted limousine windows, little cracks were forming. The strain of my mom traveling with Kirk and Candace while my dad held down the fort with Melissa and me started to show in small ways.

How could it not?

My mom went from doing macrame in the garage to managing the careers of two of the most famous kids in Hollywood, nearly overnight. My dad was now charged with learning to make dinner and managing homework in the evenings. It was no small change.

Privacy was a thing of the past, even for Melissa and me. Everyone knew our names, but even as a kid I knew the attention from folks, young and old, came with the agenda of trying to get close to Kirk and Candace. Though I reveled in it, it also took a toll.

One attempt to go to Disneyland really put the new change into perspective. Kirk was dating Alyssa Milano at the time, and soon after we arrived at the park it became impossible to move from one ride to another. We decided to just leave. Mom and Dad tried to keep things light, but we could all feel the weight of it—normal was over for the Cameron family.

My parents learned to manage some of it. If someone approached us during dinner, they would politely ask them to wait until we were done and then Kirk would oblige with photos, autographs, and conversation. Amazingly, people waited. Sometimes for hours.

My dad, head prankster of the family, looked like Kirk, so he often enjoyed being the decoy and speeding away in Kirk's Porsche while the rest of us exited to the family car. He loved fooling the paparazzi like that. It became a sort of game for all of us and was our entertainment for the evening.

Normal was over for sure.

Soon, the dangerous side of Hollywood began to emerge for me and my family. One day, the police came to the studio and wanted to talk to Kirk. Our mom asked what it was about. The police were tight-lipped about it at first, only asking Kirk and my mom if they knew anyone who drove a fancy red sports car. Kirk remembered a guy who'd come to the studio, a friend of one of the other cast members. The guy had asked Kirk if he'd mind taking a picture with him. His brother back home had cancer and thought it would really cheer him up. Kirk, always gracious, agreed. There seemed to be nothing unusual about it. Kirk took photos with people all the time.

As my mom thought about it, she realized she too had seen the fancy red sports car. A man with a young boy had arrived at our doorstep, asking if he could speak to Kirk. Feeling leery about it, Mom had said 'no,' but that she'd have Kirk call him if he would leave his phone number. The man had agreed and left with the little boy.

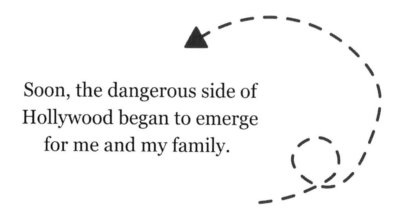

Soon, the dangerous side of Hollywood began to emerge for me and my family.

The police then explained that they believed this was the same guy they'd been looking for. The man had lured the boy into his car with an 8x10 photo of him and Kirk. The police believed there had been additional incidents with other celebrities who'd been stalked, possibly by the same man.

In an attempt to stop him, they wanted to use Kirk to lure him to the studio again. They gave this man a number to call to reserve his V.I.P. spot and gave him a special parking assignment. They told him the time of the taping, and then they waited.

The fancy red sports car drove unsuspectingly onto the lot and parked. The man was arrested immediately by undercover cops and whisked away. Most people at the studio never even knew what went down.

That incident was the catalyst that taught us a valuable lesson though—we weren't safe anymore. My parents made adjustments to how we lived and moved and who had access to us. We were lectured on safety.

Fame had arrived like a gift at our doorstep, but ironically, because of it, we had to keep the doors locked.

I was still dancing and singing in my school plays, visiting the sets to watch my brother and sister on their shows, and being generally content and fulfilled with life.

For a while, these make-believe families of *Growing Pains* and *Full House* shielded us from a harder truth that was starting to emerge within our real family: threats weren't always outside the door. My parents' relationship was crumbling by the second. Kirk was slowly being drawn into the dark world of Hollywood.

But there was someone else nearby, and He was about to stand at the door of all our hearts and knock.

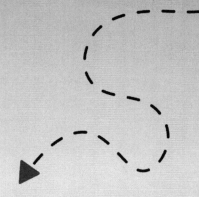

CHAPTER 4
THE NOT-SO-TV FAMILY

WHILE KIRK and Candace were depicting families America all wanted to be a part of, the harsh reality of life inside of our real family was beginning to show. These fissures were nearly undetectable at first—like when you crack a tooth. You can't see it; you just feel the pain. Later, more significant fissures would come, the kind that open the earth.

Managing Kirk's and Candace's careers had become a full-time job for my mom, while she also worked hard to continue to be the real-life mom to all of us.

For my part in the ordeal, I was causing a lot of strife in the family due to my failing grades in math. This was especially distressing to my dad who was a math teacher. Evenings were spent butting heads with him. Already tired after a long day of work and taking care of two of his four kids at night, my dad spent hours trying to teach me algebra. I understood it in the moment, but as soon as I was on my own, it converted back into something like a foreign language in my mind. I couldn't solve even the simplest of problems.

Meanwhile, the routine of a normal family of six, with all its regular stresses and strains, was something my mom and dad could only dream of now. There is no handbook for raising celebrity children. Every piece of success was met with more and more challenges. By then Kirk and Candace were worldwide celebrities, but on the home front, my parents' marriage was crumbling by the day. It wasn't long before Mom moved to an apartment by herself, partly because of the rifts in their marriage, and partly because it was more convenient for managing my siblings' careers.

They sat us down one day and Mom explained they were "separating."

"Are you divorcing?" Melissa asked.

The answers were vague. They didn't seem to know themselves what the future held. All we knew was that there was a giant chasm between them. We could feel it. They might as well have been in different states.

While Mom continued managing Kirk and Candace, we lived with Dad. Dad taught math by day and handled domestic duties at night. He was still utterly exhausted by his daughter's inability to learn math, no matter how he taught it. Our little family, the one that nobody could imagine ever splitting apart, split apart.

During this time Kirk began dating an actress whose family went to church. Her father, in fact, was the pastor of the church.

None of us had much exposure to Christianity up to that point. My mom went to church as a little girl but not beyond that. My dad had never been. The compromise between the two landed us in the "CEO" category – Christmas and Easter Only. These twice-a-year darkening-of-the-door expeditions had little to do with faith. It was simply what we did. It's what

Americans did. We paid our due diligence by making an appearance, maybe so we could be known as God-fearing people. Regardless, we never discussed the reason we went, and it never affected our daily lives. We didn't even have a manger scene in our home at Christmastime.

Funny how being ignored doesn't stop God from accomplishing His will. As we would begin to realize, His grace was abounding in our lives, and moving behind the scenes. It was about to take center stage.

It all started with Kirk's girlfriend making a simple request: "Come to church with me."

Kirk agreed to go and he sat in the pews of that church and listened. One thing stuck out to him and haunted him. The pastor asked the question: "If you died tonight, would you go to heaven?" The pastor clearly spelled out the requirements for getting into heaven—keeping the Ten Commandments. Yes, all of them.

As Kirk sat there, he knew the truth...he hadn't.

According to the pastor, that was the standard to get into heaven. Perfection.

But there was another way...a person, it turned out. The pastor shared the entire gospel, the Good News, of how God made a way by sacrificing His Son on the cross, in our place, so we could join Him in heaven. But, the pastor said, we must accept that we are sinners in need of God's saving.

Kirk drove home that night in his Porsche, weaving along the 405 in the San Fernando Valley, deep in thought about everything the pastor had said.

Eventually, he pulled into a parking lot and, for the first time in his life, talked to God. As he tells it, it was clunky and raw and genuine. He wasn't sure how he felt about God but he knew for sure he was a sinner. If grace, in the form of Jesus, was being offered, he needed it. Without Jesus, he wasn't getting into heaven.

He was seventeen at the time and at the height of his career.

Kirk didn't talk much about it at first. Instead, he kept going to church. When the relationship ended with that girlfriend, he kept going with a buddy. Then he joined a Bible study.

I, being the closest sibling to Kirk, began seeing differences. Not right away, but steadily. It wasn't the kind of conversion that knocks you off your feet and causes some kind of blinding light.

The changes were subtle, but significant. He was nicer to me. More attentive. More attuned to life around us. He'd share small things with the family sometimes, but usually he'd prefer to talk about it individually, and only if it fit naturally into the conversation.

It kept growing, though. He began paying attention to how his character, Mike Seaver, acted on the show. There were tweaks he wanted made, things he didn't feel comfortable saying anymore, ways he did and didn't want Mike Seaver to act. The writers were starting to get concerned.

Jesus was no longer something Kirk kept to himself. His growing faith began impacting all parts of his life. And it couldn't be ignored.

In the meantime, the deafening silence in our home had grown so loud it couldn't be ignored either. Dad, newly tasked with domestic duties, was trying to cook dinner for Melissa and me, do laundry, and hoping to get me graduated.

Mom too was struggling to balance it all. Really struggling.

By then, Mom had been at the apartment for a year. We kids had not adjusted to any of it.

Soon, though, Kirk began the small gesture of inviting us to church, the same way he had been invited. First he took Mom, then Dad, whose own parents hadn't wanted faith in the home when he was growing up. On and on it went, this very subtle introduction of faith into our family.

Not long after, I began attending church at Calvary Community Church in Thousand Oaks and getting involved with the youth group. One night we all went to a Michelle Pillar concert. She was a Christian singer and songwriter. I could feel my heart being moved as she sang. I knew something extraordinary was happening. I couldn't stop crying.

At the altar call, Kirk turned to me and asked, "Bridgette, do you want to go up there?"

With tears streaming down my face, I nodded. Kirk walked me up the aisle to the front, where I was led in prayer and accepted Jesus as my Lord and Savior.

From there, the rest of my family slowly followed. One by one, Jesus took us to the place of repentance and brought us under His redemptive protection. My dad, who'd always been a deep and logical thinker, was the last one to accept Christ. He asked a lot of questions and had to make sure it all lined up, but God provided those answers and spoke to his heart too. Then, in a quiet and low-key manner, which was his way, he was baptized on a men's getaway trip by Kirk. The rest of us found out after the fact.

During this time, my parents also decided to get me tested for learning disabilities. Little did we know this was going to be an answer to silent prayers from all of us, most of all my dad, who wasn't even a praying man at the time.

After a plethora of tests, the expert announced what we already knew—I had a learning disability specific to math. A severe one too. In the midst of that, he also told my parents that I had an unusual character trait—an above-average ability to see the bright side of situations and to stay positive. This partly explained how I'd managed to continue happily along in life while watching my siblings live out my dream of acting and performing. Later in life, it would not serve me perfectly, but until then, it had managed to sustain me. The tests also indicated that I was extremely creative. When I was given the Rorschach test, in which an inky black blob is presented to the subject to see what perceptions the subject has of it, I always made up a story that had a positive and unique ending rather than a negative one, despite everything I'd gone through.

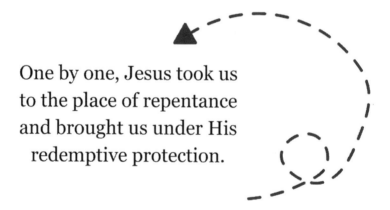

One by one, Jesus took us to the place of repentance and brought us under His redemptive protection.

It was there that my dad made a vital decision that would greatly benefit me. He did some research, then went to the school and told the administration that I had enough math to graduate and no longer needed to take additional math classes.

It was a relief to the entire family, but, of course, most of all me. Lingering in the back of my sunny outlook on life was the heavy doubt that I might be the one person in my family who wouldn't graduate from high school. With math now out of the picture, that heavy cloud dissipated.

God's merciful hand became mightier, heavier, and more evident in all our lives. Mom came home. My parents, though never divorced, returned to their marriage, and began doing the hard work they'd abandoned long ago. Now, fifty-four years later, they're still going.

My own faith began to blossom as well, but slowly. Most of my growth revolved around trying to become a whole person and heal my heart after a string of dysfunctional relationships from high school. My faith was so new. I was far from perfect, but I tried my best to honor God. I believed He didn't want me to date anyone who wasn't a Christian, so I obeyed. I went to church and tried to learn, but my focus was also still on my big dreams.

Plus, an opportunity was about to present itself that I believed would keep alive the prospect of hitting it big in the industry.

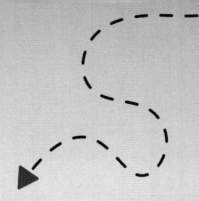

CHAPTER 5
STAND-IN

LIKE A LONG-DISTANCE RUNNER determined to finish but whose legs had given out miles back, I crawled my way to the academic finish line of high school, working my best to fulfill my dad's greatest wish for me: "Finish high school."

My siblings and I had such different academic experiences. While Melissa and I went to public high school, Candace and Kirk had to have private tutors visit their sets to accommodate their unconventional schedules. Maybe I could have benefited from private tutors, but I enjoyed the social interaction of public school and the theater opportunities it afforded me. Even though it wasn't clear I was going to pass the finish line, I was still happy. It seemed obvious to everyone including me that college wasn't in my future, but I hadn't quite worked out what exactly was.

Since second grade and all the way through high school, I had performed in plays. Before I premiered in my first blockbuster production as Daisy #1 in *Alice in Wonderland* in second grade (I still remember my one line: "I'm a daisy!"), I was writing, directing, and, of course, starring in neighborhood plays. I'd gather enough plastic fold-up chairs for all the adults, and enough kids to fill all the roles. After one very clunky rehearsal and someone stomping off like a diva at least once, we'd put on our little show for all the parents who were willing to come and sit for a whole five minutes.

I performed in dozens of dance recitals and acted in plays all the way through high school. The amazing thing about my family was that even as Kirk and Candace were rising to meteoric fame in Hollywood, they were also sitting in my high school plays, cheering me on. One night, we'd be walking the red carpet. The next day, they were watching me in *Grease*, performing as Cha Cha. This all seemed totally normal to us. My parents always made it normal. It was part of the magic of our family.

But now, here I was, on the cusp of graduating, with no actual plan for my life. I'd always assumed I'd be performing.

Then, right before graduation, an unexpected opportunity came my way. My mom approached me one night. "Bridgette, the producers of *Full House* called me. There is a stand-in opportunity on the show. They wanted to know if you'd be interested."

"A stand-in?"

Stand-ins serve an interesting function on set. They are considered crew, not cast, are called "second team" on most sets, and especially used on television shows to stand in for kids on set who need to attend school or tutoring. Since child actors are required by law to attend school for three hours a day, the second team stands in for the first team while they are attending school or tutoring.

On most shows, Mondays through Thursdays are rehearsal days for both the cast and the crew, to get lines and blocking down, lights set by the gaffer, booms out of the line of the cameras, and everything else that needs to be done. It isn't practical to stop an entire production schedule just because kids need to go to school. That's where stand-ins come in.

I couldn't believe my good fortune of being offered that position!

Because I'd been on set so often with Kirk and Candace, I already knew what to do. The stand-in's job is to rehearse lines with the actor playing opposite me, as if I were the actual actor. I learned the blocking for the character and later taught it to the actual actor. I also did anything else that was required for pre-production. Each major character had their own stand-in.

My first job was the stand-in for Andrea Barber, who played Kimmy Gibbler on *Full House*. After Andrea finished school, I met with her and taught her all the blocking I'd learned that day for each scene we'd rehearsed. For example, I might say, "Okay, you start at the top of the stairs, and then when the director yells action, you wait three seconds and then come down and say such-and-such line. You need to be at the bottom by the end of this sentence and have your conversation with DJ here." Scene by scene, line by line, I led her through what to do.

At the end of the day, either Andrea or I ran the entire show in front of all the big-wigs—the execs, the director, the producer, and any decision-makers—so they could see how it was flowing and running. Notes were given, and we'd make adjustments for the next day.

I was also there on Fridays in case something needed to be run while Andrea was in makeup or tied up elsewhere. Then, *production!* I always stayed to watch.

Besides standing in for Andrea, and later Candace—which was so fun—I also did a lot of stand-in work for guest stars like Mickey Rooney, Frankie Avalon, Annette Funicello, and the Beach Boys. As an extra I once got to do a scene with Kareem Abdul-Jabbar.

As I acquired more and more stand-in work, I came to realize how picky some directors are about who they use as stand-ins. The good stand-ins are always professional. If we are star-struck, we never show it. We arrive on time, know the etiquette on set, and are a reliable part of the crew. Thankfully, stand-ins don't need to look like the actor they are portraying. If height needs to be adjusted for an over-the-shoulder shot or for an eyeline to hit correctly, an apple box is used. I'd step up on it so the camera could practice for the right height of the actor once they came in.

One of the things I loved about Hollywood was how much the crew and talent grew to be like a real family. We spent so much time together that it truly became our home away from home. I was blessed to meet so many amazing people, famous and otherwise.

I have more memories than I can count from my time as a stand-in, but one of my favorites is the day I was doing stand-in work for Candace. The scene called for Candace and an actor to kiss. I'd been rehearsing all week with that other actor's stand-in. When it came to the kiss, we just avoided it. I didn't want to create an awkward moment of kissing a near stranger.

However, on that Thursday, the actual actor came to set and rehearsed. My goodness, he was handsome. When it came time for the kiss, I surprised the crew, the cast, the director, and most of all myself as I went for it and planted a kiss right on him!

Everyone, including the actor, burst into laughter, cheering my decision. I was equal parts proud and embarrassed by my decision. I still can't quite explain what came over me. Perhaps it was teenage impulsivity. Nevertheless, it's one of my favorite memories from my time as a stand-in.

Working in that environment had many perks. One day, Candace asked me to come to set early. I couldn't imagine what she wanted me there for, but I felt a certain excitement about it. Once I got there, it was the most terrific surprise. New Kids on the Block was there! It was a long, overdue reunion. It was so good to see them again.

I worked for *Full House* for six years and many years later was able to return to the set of *Fuller House* with my family. It was so meaningful to say hello again to Bob (Saget), John (Stamos), Lori (Loughlin) and the rest of the cast and crew.

When *Full House* ended, I immediately took a job as a stand-in for Jonathan Taylor Thomas on the show *Home Improvement*. Jonathan's mom demanded school come before acting, so I did a lot of work for Jonathan plus quite a bit for guest stars like Drew Carey.

When these shows finished for the season and took a hiatus, I'd do other projects such as commercials, movies, TV shows, pilots and more. Because I'd formed a close bond with Jonathan Taylor Thomas and his family, they asked me to be his stand-in and guardian on a movie called *Wild America*. During that time, I got to meet and work with people like Michael Chiklis and the Wayan Brothers. Through all this, I gained tons of experience in the business.

And it was at this time, well into my twenties, that my promise to God and myself to not date a non-Christian was about to be rewarded. Except God was going to have a hard time convincing me of the blessing.

By this time, I was content not being in any relationship. I knew I wanted somebody who was really on fire for the Lord, who had grown up in a Christian home, who wanted to go to church and raise a Christian family like I did.

So I kept praying for the right man to come along and for God to shut the door on the wrong one. If I saw a red flag, I would pray, "God, take 'em away as quickly as You brought them into my life if they aren't the right one for me!"

As I continued to work, this was my prayer for ten long years.

Then, one day, *he* walked in. Or more specifically, walked onto the film set where I was working. His name was John, and he worked on the crew as a grip. He was an extremely nice man as well as a shameless flirt, which didn't take away from his likability or his genuineness.

However, ringing in the back of my mind was my mom's advice: "Never date a grip. Never date anyone in the industry." It was decent advice. Film crews travel, a lot. My mom had seen firsthand on film sets the strain it could have on families.

I prayed my usual prayer and looked for red flags.

And looked. And looked. And looked.

I even implored God. "I know they're there. Show me the red flags."

But nothing. *Nada.* Not a hint of a flag anywhere.

I knew I'd see it if there was one—we were working together every single day on this film. And talking. And learning about each other. And flirting. I still couldn't find that one glaring red flag I had my eye out for. At the end of the day, he was super good guy, really cute and seemed to be everything I ever wanted.

"Lord," I'd pray at night, "if this isn't the man You have for me, then have him stop showing up on set." Yeah, I was throwing up those kinds of desperate prayers.

Nothing worked.

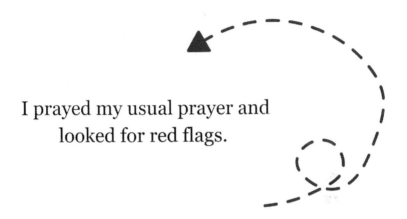

I prayed my usual prayer and looked for red flags.

Then, John asked me out. On our very first date, we talked about faith and he told me he grew up in a Christian home. Both of his parents were elders at his church, and his sister worked there part-time.

That was such a big deal for me. There he was—my future—sitting right in front of me, eating Chinese food and watching *Friends*!

Still, I was super scared about getting serious with somebody or having feelings at all. I ended up calling him one day. "This isn't normal. We need to stop seeing each other," I said.

I threw my own red flag. I broke up with him.

I was totally prepared for John to shrug his shoulders and

walk away as any guy would do. Maybe I was testing him in a way, without even realizing it.

Instead, he said, "Nope. You're not getting rid of me that fast."

I broke down crying—healing tears—and said, "That's not what you're supposed to say."

It turns out that John would end up being the best cheerleader for what was to come—including one of the biggest audition opportunities I'd received yet.

Lots of fun opportunities were coming my way. I auditioned for the movie *Planet of the Apes.* In the audition, I attempted to act like an ape, with my arms hanging long, wobbling back and forth. Meanwhile, John was filled with enough enthusiasm for both of us when he learned that Rick Baker, seven-time Academy Award-winning makeup artist (*Thriller, Exorcist, The Joker*), was involved.

Then came the opportunity of a lifetime: an audition opened for a role as a Munchkin in the Los Angeles traveling musical *The Wizard of Oz.* There couldn't have been a better opportunity for me. I am short, only 4'11. With my dance and stage experience, it was the ideal role.

But it came just as John and I were making a serious commitment to each other. He was everything I'd dreamed of in a man. If I landed the role, it meant months away from him. John was nothing but supportive, though, and encouraged me to do it. That's when I knew I could love this guy forever and that he would do whatever it took to make our relationship work. "We'll work around it," he assured me.

I went to the audition at a dance studio. We split into groups. One group would go over to the piano and learn the song they gave us. The other went elsewhere to learn the dance.

Then we would swap. Finally, we came together to perform it in front of the decision-makers.

After one of the performances, the choreographer came up to me and said, "I'd like you to come with me." She took me to the back corner of the room while everybody else was still rehearsing. In the back, the choreographer taught me a totally different dance to a completely different song. I learned it very quickly and did very well. The choreographer looked at me and said, "You're very, very good. A very fast learner."

A huge smile crossed my face. I couldn't hold it back. "This is it!" I told myself.

Afterward, a man approached me and said, "Well, you ready to go on tour? Because you nailed that audition." I couldn't believe the enthusiasm that was coming my way. After all, I'd gotten used to a lot of rejection in my life for any roles other than stand-ins.

I called John. "I really think this is going to be my time," I told him. "I'm going to get picked. I can feel it!" I must've rambled on for twenty minutes about all the details, all the compliments, all the ways I felt so good about how I'd performed.

I was sure things were going to turn around for me. When I auditioned for other shows, there was always something that didn't feel quite right about them. I never knew why, but I never felt devastated that I didn't get the part. I always saw it coming. Something had told me, "Not this one." Or as Mom used to say, "Iris said 'no' today."

But this audition felt right. It felt perfect. I could feel it in my bones. This was meant to be. *The Wizard of Oz* had everything that I loved to do. It was singing, it was dancing, it was acting, it was traveling, it was a musical and being part of a cast. And I was a shoo-in.

I knew I'd have to leave *Full House* and *Home Improvement* if I got the part, but that was okay. When it's time to go, it's time to go.

The Wizard of Oz was calling my name. It wasn't just a dream. It was *the* dream.

I waited for my agent to call with the good news.

Mom and me.

With Kirk on my first birthday.

With Melissa and Mom on Easter.

With Candace at the beach.

With Melissa at Zumba Beach.

Dad and his girls.

Dad, Uncle David, and Rusty Rock do handstands.

That's me!

With my childhood friend, KK, riding the waves.

Lifeguard tower 12 at Zumba Beach.

We loved swimming.

With Kirk on Christmas morning.

Candace, Melissa, me and Kirk.

Riding Big Wheels with Kirk.

Singing away!

With Melissa, singing into our Donny and Marie
microphones.

Second grade Alice in Wonderland play. I'm a daisy!

More from the Alice in Wonderland play.

Me in Fiddler on the Roof.

With childhood best friend, Heather, then and now.

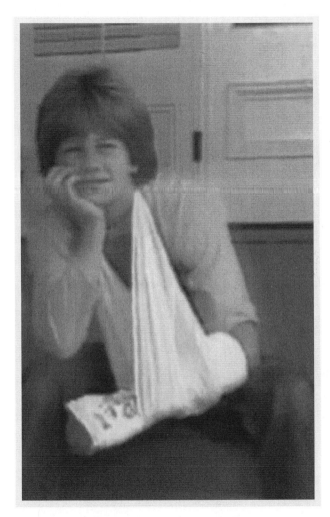

Kirk's modified Kool-Aid commercial.

Kirk's 16th birthday.

Mom, Dad and Iris Burton.

The girls with Dad at the Youth and Film Awards.

Me, Kirk, Candace and Melissa at a BOP magazine event.

When Kirk presented at the People's Choice Awards.

Kirk with Phyllis Diller, Lucille Ball, Emmanuel Lewis and President
Ronald Reagan.

The whole Cameron family: Mom, Barbara; Kirk; Melissa; Candace; Bridgette; Father, Robert. ★

TURNS SWEET 16!

You're Invited To **BRIDGETTE CAMERON'S** Party!

Kirk is sure proud of sister Bridgette. You can see it in his face! ★

Wow! It was *so* exciting to be at Bridgette's Sweet 16! She looked *gorgeous* . . . and Kirk was *exceptionally* handsome! Now *SuperTeen*'s sharing this once-in-a-lifetime event with *you!*

Sean Astin, Kirk's co-star in *Like Father, Like Son,* has a warm hug for Bridgette. Lucky girl! ★

A vision in white: Kirk and Alan Thicke have a warm off-screen relationship, isn't that neat? ★

My Sweet 16 announcement in BOP magazine.

Bridgette Cameron

My senior photo.

BOP magazine New Kids on the Block debut party.

The Knight brothers with the Cameron sisters.

Jonathan Knight, New Kids on the Block concert.

New Kids on the Block on the set of Fuller House.

With Michael J. Fox.

With Frankie Avalon, years after first working together.

Our wedding day: May 6, 2000. Married in the church from 7th Heaven.

Our family visiting Cadillac Ranch.

The last photo before the accident. We made it to Texas!

May 27, 2015 … the accident.

At the K-LOVE awards with Kirk, Chelsea, and John.
The day after the accident.

At the K-LOVE awards with TobyMac.

As Stand-in during filming for Farmer and the Belle.

On the Farmer and the Belle: Saving Santaland set.

With choreographer and dance partner Van Spencer.

1st Place, Audience Choice and 3rd Place, Charity.

On the set of Fuller House with Candace and Bob Saget.

With Jonathan Taylor Thomas from Home Improvement.

With Zachary Ty Bryan from Home Improvement.

Revisiting my childhood home.

My family today.

All of us with Mom and Dad. Still Blessed, and no one overlooked!

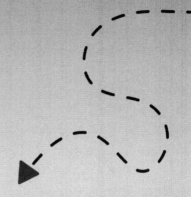

CHAPTER 6
BROKEN

TO UNDERSTAND my life up to this point—and what God intended for it—you must understand the jaw saga. Let's rewind a bit.

That little girl who stood at the wall of the Who's-Who of Hollywood kid actors, who gave her everything for the great and mighty Iris Burton, who kept kindling hope like the entire flame depended on her unending excitement and enthusiasm… that girl still struggled through braces.

In second grade, shortly after "Iris said 'no' today," I got my first set. I had an extreme underbite, where my bottom jaw came out and my top jaw went behind my bottom teeth. So starting in second grade, I had fourteen teeth extracted over several years and braces put on. But that's not all.

I also got rubber bands put on…and a neck brace. I was born with a spine disorder called kyphosis, which caused a hunch in my back. This brace, which I wore nearly twenty-four-seven, ran from my neck to my hips.

That neck brace, more than the teeth braces, made me

nervous walking into second grade. Would Doug, my second-grade crush who told my mom he wanted to marry me, still be interested once he saw it?

Despite the fear of the neck brace, the teeth braces stuck around much longer.

Third grade, I still wore them.

Fourth grade, I still wore them.

Fifth grade.

Sixth grade.

Seventh grade.

Eighth grade.

Ninth grade.

Tenth grade.

Eleventh grade.

Senior year...still wore them.

Every single picture of me, from second grade to senior year, shows me in braces. While my brother's Hollywood posters were hanging in girls' rooms all across the nation, and Candace seemed to bring glamor to every picture that was snapped of her, I was popping rubber bands across the room, digging food out of wherever it was lodged, and checking the mirror to make sure nothing was stuck to the front of my teeth.

For ten years.

By that time, my teeth were straight. The plan was for the braces, rubber bands, and headgear to correct my underbite as I grew, so they stayed on and on and on.

Before my senior portraits, I went to my mom and told her I wanted to take my top braces off.

"I don't have a single picture of me without braces, and I don't want my senior pictures to show me with braces on in the yearbook."

To my great relief, she agreed. She didn't fight me on it at all.

But as soon as my portraits were made, my braces went right back on. This brought about a lightbulb moment for me that none of the dentists seemed to have—if my teeth weren't fixed by now, after ten years, was it possible they weren't going to be fixed with braces?

Again, I talked to my parents about it and asked for them to be removed once and for all this time, and to my surprise, they agreed. We took the braces off.

Life was good without braces! And my teeth seemed to be doing just fine.

My love life had even blossomed.

And then I found myself there at the audition of a lifetime, the audition that would make all my dreams come true: *The Wizard of Oz!*

Up until this point, my teeth served as a perfect metaphor for my life. I suppose I could break it down one crooked tooth at a time, but the bottom line was that, even though I kept a smile on my face, my life was like my jaws—nothing fit like it was supposed to. Without some kind of radical surgery from the Lord, nothing was ever going to fit in my life.

But this audition could change that! I had a feeling that God was setting everything right.

I went in there and gave it everything I had. It couldn't have gone better. I danced with all the confidence and passion I had. I felt like a pro and barely broke a sweat, not to mention, I was under five-foot tall, perfect Munchkin height. Everything was coming together.

My agent finally called.

"Bridgette," she said, "you didn't get it."

Breathless, like I had taken a punch to the stomach, I

thought maybe I misunderstood. "What do you mean I didn't get it?"

Agents have the awful job of calling their clients and breaking bad news. Like cops and firefighters who pull up to car accident after car accident, they learn to remain detached from the emotion that's going to come.

But this...this was shocking for both of us. She had no explanation. The decision-makers gave no explanation, even as I was vomiting out shock.

"But they said I did great. The choreographer pulled me aside! Taught me my own dance! Told me I was really good at it..." My words trailed off as tears took over.

"I don't know, Bridgette. I'm sorry."

Why?

Why, why, why?

I wanted to know so badly. *WHY?* Maybe if I could get the *why*, I could find out why my whole life's dreams were still turning out as crooked and disjointed as my teeth.

God! Why aren't You letting me have my dream?

The cheery, always positive, bounce-back gal named Bridgette Cameron was not bouncing back.

That inky black blob the psychologist had shown me all those years before, the one that I could imagine a good ending for every single time, was now just a black blob of despair.

I seemed to be inching along toward an awful conclusion— there wasn't going to be a good ending. No victory march. No "she finally did it!" moment. No win.

Every single door to my dream was closing...even the ones that looked certain I should walk through. They were slamming in my face and without a hint of an explanation—not from the casting director, not from God, not from anyone.

Unbelievably, or maybe not, the jaw saga continued. I started having health issues and noticed my bottom jaw slowly started to protrude out again. I'd learned through the process that the jaw is a bone with a memory, much like muscle memory. It began to slip back into its original position.

I stopped digesting food properly because I couldn't chew my food correctly.

Maybe if I could get the *why*,
I could find out why my whole
life's dreams were still
turning out as crooked
and disjointed as my teeth.

One night I talked with John. I told him that I didn't want to live my entire adult years with my jaw protruding and an underbite that caused me all kinds of problems. He was supportive of my decision. I visited my orthodontist to discuss it. She informed me that in order to correct the problem completely, I was looking at jaw surgery. She told me I would also need braces for two more years.

I found an oral surgeon named Dr. Peter Scheer. The "jaw surgery" plan, as it turned out, was going to be way more complicated than I'd imagined. He explained the process like he was explaining an oil change, except it involved maneuvers like breaking my jaw and other "minor" stuff like that.

The surgery would widen my upper jaw and push my lower jaw backward so my teeth would fit together correctly. He also believed my chin was too long and wanted to shave some of the chin bone off.

Surgery came right before Halloween. It went as planned. Dr. Scheer even exclaimed that the piece of bone he'd taken from my jaw fit perfectly to fill in the separation the surgery had created in my cheeks. He declared the surgery a success.

The recovery, however, was not quite as exciting. My jaw was wired shut for over four months. I would be drinking all my meals (which were basically protein shakes) through a syringe.

I was in bed on major pain pills when Halloween arrived. John, being the fun-loving guy he is, thought it would be fun to carve a pumpkin in my honor, complete with wire hangers protruding out of my jaw. While I thought John's idea for my pumpkin was cute, I was barely well enough to go into the kitchen to watch him carve it. He posted a picture of the final result on my Facebook page. My friends were relieved to hear I was doing well and had such a good sense of humor about the healing process.

My days were spent creating my own sign language and weird grunts to try and communicate what I needed. I could relate quite a bit to the figure in the Bible named Zechariah, Elizabeth's husband, who was suddenly struck mute until his son John the Baptist was born.

The recovery, to put it mildly, was arduous. From the bottom of my eye sockets all the way across my face, ear to ear, and all the way down my chin, I was completely numb. I could not feel a thing. My doctor had warned me about this and told me that he couldn't guarantee I'd get all feeling back.

The feeling in my face eventually began to return in a strange kind of tapping sensation along my cheekbones. The doctor told me it was my nerves waking up. I decided to help them, tapping around on my face daily to remind them they had an obligation to get back to work.

The day I got my jaw unwired, we celebrated with friends. I ate pasta and sorbet. It was amazing! I regained full feeling in my face and though the recovery process was difficult, it was well worth it in the end, and I don't regret the surgery at all. I would recommend it to those struggling with the same condition I did.

But my entertainment dreams, those were still wired shut.

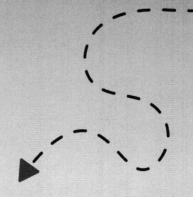

CHAPTER 7
THE FIRST MIRACLE

THE THING about life is that it always carries on, with or without dreams coming true. And sometimes life brings different kinds of fulfillment. John and I got married in May of 2000 and started a family right away, something we both very much wanted. I became a mom for the first time, and I could not have been happier. The thrill of holding my son, Cameron, couldn't be matched by anything.

But even with the fulfillment of being a mother, something in me still wanted to try and juggle both a new baby and a career. I'd hook anyone willing in my family to come babysit while I'd go to this or that audition whenever I could.

Finally, my mom confronted me.

"Bridgette," my mom said, "I want to be a grandmother, not a full-time babysitter."

If my jaw saga wasn't the end of it all, this, I knew, was the death knell to my entertainment career. John and I talked, agreeing we had to leave the entertainment industry for good.

John found a more stable job, and I became a stay-at-home mom.

Somewhere still, though, was that longing, that hope, that dream that hadn't left me since childhood. Instead of dealing with it openly and outwardly like any good therapist would ask you to, I buried it deep inside of me, and never spoke of it again. Soon came our second son, Everett. The new feeling of welcoming another child *and* a sibling for our oldest son, Cameron, filled John and me with so much joy.

Life got hectic after that, raising two small boys. We did life like most Americans, cramming activities and fun into every nook and crannied space of our lives. But we enjoyed every minute of it, and I realized something I didn't quite know about myself: Motherhood was my greatest calling. It suited me too. I'd always wanted to be a mom, and I'd always wanted a family, but just how much motherhood would mean to me, well, that exceeded all other expectations.

With two boys, John and I now dreamed of having a little girl. It would complete our family circle in the best of ways. John joked that I should have twins. Twins run in our family, but I didn't give it much thought or credence. Already having two boys, the thought of having two babies at one time seemed like it might do me in...or make me a crazier than I already was!

Soon enough, we were pregnant. I was so thrilled. My two energetic boys were filling my life with toy trucks, LEGO bricks and sheet forts. Life was going well, and so was my pregnancy, but I was a bit more tired this time around.

One afternoon I took the boys to Target, where all moms go to entertain toddlers and themselves. John was out of town for work, so the boys needed an extra bit of entertaining that day. We headed up and down aisles, mostly aisles I wanted to go down, trying to avoid the toy section at all costs. Baby Everett, wide-eyed and content, sat in his car seat. Cameron, now a toddler, got restless, so we played a game where I let him bump me a little in the back with the cart. I'd be dramatic about it (still trying to live the dream!). We were having a great time.

Finally, it was time to go home. The boys needed a nap and so did I. With both boys, I'd had the normal first-nine-weeks fatigue, but this little was really taking it out of me in a different way. I put the boys down for their naps and crashed onto the couch in a deep sleep.

I woke up with no concept of how much time had passed but with an overwhelming sense of panic. I sat up and suddenly felt it, the feeling that every pregnant woman fears—a *gush* before the baby is supposed to come. I sat stunned. Frozen. I knew what I'd just felt. Only one question came to mind.

Am I having a miscarriage?

I gasped, jumped up, ran to my bathroom, screaming inside, begging God before I knew what to even say. *Please, God, no. Please don't let this happen.*

My worst fears were confirmed. Blood. Lots of it. I began cramping. I had my phone with me, so I called John.

Before he could say anything, I blurted it out. "I think I'm having a miscarriage. I've got to go to the hospital."

The room spun around me as we worked out how to get me to the hospital. John was too far away to take me. I told him I'd figure it out but that he should start heading there right away. The whole conversation was a blur.

I called my neighbor and asked if she and her husband could come over.

"I need to go now," I said, though surely the panicked tone of my voice said more than my words.

As I waited in the bathroom, I tried cleaning myself up. It seemed futile. As I looked at the toilet paper, tears streaming down my face, I saw what looked like a baby.

It was surreal, like everything you might see in a medical book. Tiny hands. Tiny, webbed feet. Sunken eyes that looked like a gummy bear.

There was nothing else on the toilet paper. In fact, it was white as snow, a perfect, angelic bed for this little one who lay right in its center.

At that very moment, I felt God say, *This is your daughter. You need to say goodbye.*

No. *No! I want to put her back, God! I want to put her back! Put her back!*

But only God's gentle word to me was left: *You need to say goodbye.*

Alone in the bathroom, I did just that.

I called my mom, and through anguished tears, told her I'd had a miscarriage.

My mom had the strangest reaction though. She just calmly said, "Okay."

Okay?

Then she said, "Bridgette, whatever you do, whenever you get to the hospital, please, please, please do not let them do a D&C until you have an ultrasound. Refuse to go back to that operating room until they do an ultrasound *in your room.*"

I didn't fully understand the reasoning for her instructions, but they were so specific that I couldn't deny them. Still, here I was, holding my tiny baby in my hand.

"But Mom, these are doctors and nurses and..."

"Do not leave that room for the operating room until you get that ultrasound," she repeated. She'd heard too many stories, she explained.

I wasn't in the mood to argue so I just said, "Okay." She told me she was on her way. She'd be there in three hours.

I cleaned myself up, wrapped my baby in the toilet paper and got into the car with my neighbor. Her husband stayed to watch my boys. On the way to the hospital, I called my doctor and he said, "Why don't you come over to my office. Let me examine you first."

His office was next door to the hospital. To my eternal disappointment, he was a different doctor than the ones who delivered my boys. Cameron's doctor was in West Hills. We had moved after that. Everett's doctor had been beyond wonderful, a dream for any nervous, anxious, or worn-out mom. But before this pregnancy, she had left labor and delivery. My insurance assigned me to Dr. Parker this time, who was everything an expectant mom hopes a doctor isn't. His bedside manner was atrocious. He seemed mechanical and uninterested in anything that concerned his patient.

I lay on the table waiting for him, staring at the ceiling in disbelief. He blew in with all the warmth of a deep freezer. He turned toward the table, stopped, and looked down.

"You got blood on my shoes," he stated, then looked around like the mess on the ground was more concerning than the mess on the table. It seemed as though that's all patients were—messes to clean up and get out the door with the garbage.

"You're bleeding a lot," he continued to mumble, like an afterthought, like there wasn't a woman, desperate and frightened, who'd just lost her child. "I don't know what's going on. I'm sending you to the hospital next door."

If I could've run out of that room, I would've. I made it to the hospital with the help of my neighbor and got into a room immediately. As my mom had warned, they began prepping me for surgery.

"I want an ultrasound," I blurted.

The nurse dutifully continued with her task. "Don't worry, they'll do one."

"No. In this room. I want an ultrasound before you take me to the OR."

Unflustered, she clipped on my bracelet and gave me a pitiful smile. "Honey, you'll get it."

"I'm not leaving this room until I get an ultrasound."

She looked me in the eyes. "Ma'am, listen, I—"

At that moment, John walked into the room, catching us both by surprise. "My wife isn't going anywhere until you get her that ultrasound."

The nurse nodded, but I caught an eye roll as she turned. I took a deep breath and tried to hold in my tears. John walked to my bedside. He seemed to be the first compassionate person I'd seen in a while. Seeing him brought a good dose of emotional relief, though the dam of my grief had already started to break. I listened on repeat to myself in that bathroom saying goodbye to this...this daughter. God had said *daughter.* Despite my best efforts, the tears still flowed.

John gently laid his hands on my belly and began to pray. I don't remember the exact prayer, but he prayed for the baby. Over and over, he prayed.

For a long time, we waited in that cold room, with nothing to hold on to but God. Nobody was in a rush. It seemed the entire medical team had resigned itself to what happened. Now they just had to follow through with standard miscarriage procedures, except they were also having to deal with an unco-operative patient.

But my mom's voice kept ringing in my ears to make sure they gave me an ultrasound in my room. Even more than her words, the *urgency* with which she had said them gripped me.

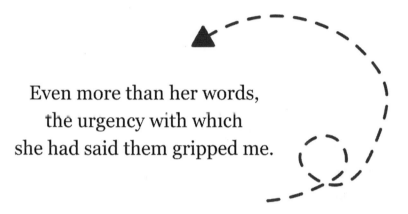

Even more than her words,
the urgency with which
she had said them gripped me.

Finally, the ultrasound technician came in, wheeling her cart, matter-of-factly squirting the jelly on my stomach, and getting her machine ready. John held my hand on the other side of the bed. In the deepest part of myself that I could reach, I prepared to see the womb empty of a fluttering heartbeat. God had told me to say goodbye.

The tech swirled the jelly with the wand, her face grim with the anticipation of the inevitable. My eyes darted back and forth between the monitor and her expression, waiting for— dreading—the words she would speak.

But her expression twisted into something I hadn't expected...confusion. Her brows furrowed, her gaze less on me or my belly and more on the monitor, the buttons. It was like her entire attention had been swallowed up by one singular thing as she stared at the screen.

She finally looked at me. Then at the monitor. Then back at me, her eyes widening by the second.

"What?!" I finally cried out, desperate to know what happened. "What is it?"

"You're still pregnant," she whispered, almost like she didn't believe it herself.

We all looked at the monitor, but she'd removed the wand from my belly.

Hot tears of anger rushed down my face. I felt my cheeks flush. "How dare you say that to me!"

John tried to reach for me, but I yanked myself away from him.

"How dare you! I miscarried my baby at home! I held her in my hands!"

In a calm voice, she put the wand back on my belly. "You're still pregnant. Look."

We all looked at the screen and there, in the middle of the sack, was a tiny, fluttering, heartbeat.

For the first time during this entire event, John started crying. My tears kept flowing too, but the anger had vanished into something else: shock. Even the tech was crying.

At that moment, my mom walked in. As moms do, she rushed to my bedside, wanting to scoop her child into her arms and comfort her. "Oh Bridgette, I'm so sorry. I'm so, so sorry." She fumbled for more words. No one in my family had ever experienced a miscarriage so the words were coming harder for her, but her mom's heart was there, grieving with me.

I had to stop her. "Mom, I'm still pregnant."

"What?" she gasped.

And now she was looking at the monitor too.

Even as the evidence was beating right in front of me, I couldn't get over what I had experienced in the bathroom. I poured it all out to my mom. "I don't understand what's going on. I miscarried. God told me to say goodbye to my daughter. I held her in my hands, Mom."

Mom nodded, trying to understand it all along with me. "Let's wait and see what the doctor says," she said in the calm way only a mom can muster in a crisis.

I was already prepped for surgery, with a catheter in. So, we just sat there and waited for the doctor.

Finally, Dr. Parker came in, as unmoved and expressionless as he'd been when I had gotten blood on his shoes earlier. He stood at the end of the bed, the furthest distance he could stand from a patient, and reviewed my chart without making eye contact with me.

"I don't know what's going on with you," he shrugged, flipping through papers in my chart. "Obviously you're not going to have a D&C today."

"Okay," I said, "but what is happening?"

"I don't know. I've never seen anything like this. We'll keep you overnight to monitor you and probably send you home tomorrow."

"But what's going to happen to the baby?" I asked.

"I don't know. Either your body is going to hold on to it, or your body is going to reject it and push it out."

He left us staring at one another, in shock.

The next day, I was sent home. I lay on the couch, with Mom and John hovering over me. My mind raced through the events of the previous day, over and over—what I had seen, personally witnessed, and felt sure God had said to me. It all felt surreal.

At one point, Mom sat on the couch with me, stroking my feet. "You know, Bridgette, it wouldn't be a bad idea to get a second opinion."

I looked at her and nodded.

I called my old OB/GYN and with desperation clearly in my voice, asked her if she'd see me. She agreed.

After a brief exam, she told me she'd like to send me to a specialist. Within a couple of days, I was lying in his office as he glided that all-too-familiar wand across my belly. Finally, he looked at me with deep compassion.

"Bridgette, you were having twins."

I could hardly breathe. "Twins?"

"Yes. Identical twins." He waited a beat. "Do twins run in your family?"

"My dad is a twin."

He turned the monitor toward me. "There were two sacks and one placenta. One sack is empty. The other sack has the heart beating. This baby looks healthy. That's a healthy heart-beat, for sure. We just can't determine yet what this baby is going to do. I really can't say what will happen at this point, but I can definitely say these were twins."

FOR THE NEXT FEW WEEKS, grief followed me around, but it was mixed with joy at the same time. Strange bedfellows, those two. I celebrated the life inside me. I grieved the one who'd left too soon. Those emotions became my constant companions.

Fear often tried to join the club. I tried not to play the "what-ifs" in my head, but I couldn't help but wonder if the silly little game that Cameron and I had played in Target with the shopping cart had contributed to it all.

I knew most likely not. Babies are resilient and a knock to the back from a toddler with a shopping cart was a small thing compared to the other obstacles little lives navigate, most unbeknownst to us.

At the next ultrasound, they asked if we'd like to know the sex of the baby. We'd kept it a surprise for the first two, but for this child, we were really hoping for a sister for Cameron and Everett. After all, John had prayed for twin girls, and God had told me this was a girl.

The ultrasound would be the ultimate confirmation.

When we walked into the waiting room after the ultrasound was complete, my mother-in-law stood when she saw us. We tried to keep our expressions as neutral as possible as we asked to get my mom on the phone. When Mom answered, we all huddled around the speaker phone. I could hardly contain my joy.

"It's a girl!" I announced.

I don't think there was a single dry eye in our crowd.

A little while after that, my mom came out to stay with me. One day we were sitting on the couch chatting and she said, "You know, Bridgette, now that you know you're having a girl, you also know that the baby you lost would have been a girl since they were identical twins. Maybe it's time to bring closure and give that little girl a name to celebrate her life too."

John and I gave it some thought. There was a winery we really loved in Napa, the Francis Ford Coppola winery. Francis Ford Coppola was a legendary filmmaker and one of the wines from his vineyard had become a favorite of ours: the Sofia, named after his daughter. With our family's long history in the entertainment industry, the backstory gave me even more reason to love the name. I floated the idea by John, and he agreed.

We named our daughter who had passed away Sofia. Her birthday was August 8, 2005. Every year we celebrate her. I went on to have a normal pregnancy with our second daughter. In March of 2006, Reese, a healthy baby girl, was born.

Years later, when Reese was four, she and I were sitting in the rocking chair where I'd nursed all my children. We were playing horsey and having fun when she stopped suddenly and looked me right in the eyes. "Mommy, do I have a sister?"

My heart stopped, then started pounding. We knew someday we'd need to talk to Reese about what happened, but we thought it should be when she was much older.

"Why do you ask me that?"

"Mommy, there is this little girl who comes to me in my dreams. She wants to talk with me and play with me."

"Do you see her a lot?" I asked.

"All the time," she said.

I could hardly comprehend what Reese was telling me.

"And," Reese added emphatically, "she looks just like me."

I was stunned into temporary silence, staring into her curious eyes. How could she know this? No one would have said anything to her about what had happened all those years ago.

I chose my words carefully, holding back tears. "You do have a sister."

"I do?" Her eyes widened even more.

"Her name is Sofia." I went on to explain, in the best way I could to a child, that I'd had two babies in my stomach, but Sofia went to heaven before she was born.

Soon after, in kindergarten, Reese was given the assignment, along with all the kids, to tell the class about their family using LEGO bricks. Reese completed the task, stood up, and introduced her family—including her sister, Sofia, who, she explained, was in heaven.

That afternoon the teachers pulled me aside to let me know, a little worried about who Sofia was. They thought Reese might have a new, imaginary friend. I laughed and told them the story. They were amazed and touched by Reese's understanding and love for her sister. They hadn't known about the miscarriage.

This wasn't the end of it. Reese would go on to tell anyone who would listen about Sofia. She was proud to have a sister, and even strangers got to hear about her.

Reese grew up to be very creative. She'd create videos where she'd film herself on camera and then use a filter to split the screen and film herself on the other side of it too. She explained that this other side of the split screen was her sister Sofia. They'd look alike, of course, but be wearing different outfits, as twins might. These two girls she depicted on video would have conversations, tell jokes, and act out scenes they might really have experienced together had Sofia been given more time with us here on earth.

Sometimes not having Sofia by her side in real life would make Reese cry. She'd watch out the window and see her two brothers, who were close in age, playing. She loved them but wished she had her sister to play with too.

John and I would sit and watch Reese as she moved about her daily life, marveling at this little miracle. We agreed that Reese seemed to have the personality of two people, always so vibrant and charismatic, marveling at the way she seemed to fill up a room. Her consciousness of Sofia never seemed to grow into an unhealthy obsession, but rather bloomed into a deep love for her sister.

This extraordinary event began to grow my faith as I watched. I felt God draw me into an idea, one that felt strange at first: I should do more than just *believe* in God and *trust* Jesus as my savior. God wanted me to get to *know* Him. Spend time with Him. Read His Word. Pray.

I was busy, though. I had three small children. Still, I gave it effort. I journaled here and there, went to Bible studies, joined women's groups, and attended church regularly.

There was nothing wrong with any of those things, but it still didn't feel like the core of what I was longing for in my faith.

God wasn't done with me yet. Not by a long shot. He had more for me, and as God does, He delivers miracles and messages in the most unexpected of ways.

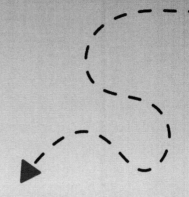

CHAPTER 8
MIRACLE ON A HIGHWAY

"WE CAN SEE GOD'S COUNTRY!" one of us joked as we made plans to drive cross country from Palm Springs, California, to Nashville, Tennessee. My brother, Kirk, had been asked to host the K-LOVE Awards, and it was the same year the Christmas movie we'd made together, *Saving Christmas,* was up for some awards. Kirk invited us to come, so of course our family jumped at the chance to go.

Cameron was now fourteen, Everett was twelve, and Reese was nine. Driving from California to Nashville would take a solid four days, but we made it a family road trip. On a sunny California morning, we all piled into the car, eager for our adventure. Growing up, we'd always road-tripped together as a family. Mom packed cereal and drinks in a cooler. Dad, a middle school P.E. teacher, made us do exercises at every rest stop. We listened to shows on tape. These trips held some of my best memories and I wanted that for my family now.

Our adventure stopped as quickly as it started, however, thanks to the flashing lights of a California Highway patrolman who reminded us to slow down. Didn't he know how eager we were to get on with our adventure?

We promised him we would and off we went again, ready to make memories.

As we made our way east on I-40, I marveled at the changes of scenery. We passed the Mojave National Preserve, then drove through Flagstaff, Arizona (which boasted many signs that made it nearly impossible to pass on the chance to see the Grand Canyon National Park), Albuquerque, New Mexico, with its desolate deserts, and then into the panhandle of Texas, which had its own unique feel, though it seemed more desolate than even New Mexico.

It's mostly a boring drive, with little to look at and few places to stop. The populations of most towns linger below 500, and anything of interest was boarded up long ago. Those who have stayed have done so for reasons most of us can't understand.

Despite the lack of entertainment for much of the way, we Ridenours are fantastic at entertaining ourselves. First, we stopped for lunch at Cracker Barrel. John and Reese decided to play a quick game of checkers on the porch with the rocking chairs. Next, we came upon the iconic Cadillac Ranch in Amarillo, where the smell of spray paint hit us almost as hard as the red dirt carried by the wind of the Plains. We were 200 miles from Oklahoma City, which was over the halfway point of our trip.

With lots of pride, we made our own spray paint mark at Cadillac Ranch. Then, with full bellies, we carried on. Everett sat in the front seat with John, and I joined Cameron in the back. Reese sat in the third row. Ahead was a handful of small

Texas and Oklahoma towns we would forget as soon as we passed through them.

As we entered the west side of Groom, Texas, on Route 66, we noticed a wall of dirt moving toward us. It was thin at first, like a light fog, very similar to a low moving bank of clouds... except not quite.

It was noticeable enough that the car grew quiet. We marveled at it for a bit.

Pellets of dirt hit the car like hail, except moving sideways from our right.

The dirt got thicker.

The visibility got lower.

"A dust storm," John guessed, glancing back at me, and I agreed. We were familiar with the phenomenon in California, though we hadn't experienced one this severe. We would later call it by the name that it's known by around the world: *haboob*.

The phenomenon is caused by the collapse of a thunderstorm. A downburst creates a straight-line wind gust, sometimes traveling as fast as 60 miles an hour, that can be pressed low to the ground by the cold air from evaporating rain. It gathers up silt and rain into a wall of fury that arrives as dust and dirt.

This is what we'd now come face to face with. Where there had been light, darkness began swallowing it up.

We drove a little farther. John's grip tightened on the steering wheel. The conversations lulled. Unlike how fog tends to reflect and encase light, the taillights of cars ahead disappeared.

"Something's not right," John uttered, loud enough for me to hear, soft enough that perhaps the kids didn't pick up on it. I glanced back at Reese. Her eyes were fixed nervously on the windshield.

I felt the speed of the car dramatically slow. We'd been going seventy miles an hour. We were now at twenty. Within seconds the visibility diminished even more. Dirt slammed against our car. The sound was like the heavy slapping brushes of a car wash, hardly damaging but already creating a layer of fine dust across our windshield and an incessant, disturbing noise that was hard to ignore.

"You should pull over," I said to John.

"No. No, I can't. You can't stop on a highway. You *never* stop on a highway."

That, I knew, was true. But we couldn't see very well, and it was hard to tell which was more dangerous: to continue driving or to park on the side of the road.

John tried the wipers, but they just squeaked across the windshield like it was dry earth.

Suddenly, we screeched to a halt as John caught flashing hazards of a semi-truck fully stopped ahead. We were separated by only a couple feet. My breath caught in my throat, but I'd been a mom for a while. I'd trained myself not to fully panic when kids were nearby.

I could only see John's profile, but I knew the color had drained from his face.

Then, as if a thick and low cloud had descended, everything around us went dark. All the normal sounds of the road faded away. It was quiet, except for the wind and the dirt.

Seconds later, before I could voice any additional concern, John said, "We've got to pull off the road."

Something in his eyes made me totally trust him. I knew he was making decisions with the God we both trusted.

John slowly pulled the car to the right of the semi, onto the shoulder of the road. We were now in the direct path of the storm's brutal wind and dirt.

The kids started to ask questions, but I indicated they should settle down. Instinctively they did.

We sat there, wondering, anxious, encased in this weird cloud of dirt. I noticed John's hands. One remained on the steering wheel though we were stopped, as if he might change his mind any second. His eyes darted from the rearview mirror to the side mirror to the back of the semi, but for no apparent reason. None of us could see a thing.

The wind whistled through the cracks in the car. Everything was dark, like the sun had simply decided to leave.

I let out a tense breath and was about to offer a quick smile of relief when out of the corner of my eye, I saw it: a flash of metal.

The sound of rubber tires on the concrete filled the vacuum of soundlessness.

I didn't have time to scream. It wouldn't have been heard anyway.

An explosion rocked everything from our car to my eardrums.

Another semi, just as large as the first one, slammed right into the back of the one beside us, exactly where we'd just been just seconds before. A fireball shot straight into the dark sky and past John's window. Shocking heat swept against my left cheek.

God spoke to me and told me to get Reese into the seat next to me. I instructed her in a tense but calm voice and then buckled her in.

We both trembled.

Seconds later, we were all violently thrust forward. The car lurched in a way I didn't know a car could. A horrific screeching of metal on metal filled our ears as another semi wedged itself between our car and the burning semis on our left side.

Another fire exploded, the light intense against the dark curtain of dirt that had enveloped us all. I was screaming, though I didn't want to. John was saying something to the kids, but it was like I was in a tunnel far away. His eyes were wide with a panic I'd never seen in them.

Then all went silent.

My whole body began to shake. John clawed at his door, but it was jammed shut, the second semi wedged against his door.

More heat, intense heat. I sat frozen, aware of Reese next to me, but unable to control what I was doing or feeling. It felt like the whole world was on fire and we were in the middle of it.

Something kicked in, and I grabbed my phone. It's what anyone does in an emergency—calls 9-1-1.

It seemed all sound had vanished from the world. My ears rang with nothing but terror.

My attention snapped to the front windshield. A man slid across the hood of our car.

"Get out! Get out!" the man yelled. "Get out of the car! Fire!"

The kids' screams began. It was hard to hear what else he was saying, but his expression said it all. This was life-or-death.

John pointed to my door. The smoke was choking now, and I could barely see anything.

I grabbed for the handle, and it opened. I quickly whisked the kids out, but we were engulfed in black smoke and the cloak of dirt that wouldn't leave us.

"Over here!"

The voice was faint. Unfamiliar.

"Over here!"

We turned but didn't know to what or whom.

"Over here, this way!"

I gathered the kids. We could barely see each other through the fog of dust and smoke.

Their eyes were so round, so scared. I tried to steady my next words and make them count. They needed to hear this and obey it, without question. I looked at each of them for no more than a half-second.

"Run," I said, though it almost sounded like a whisper. *Run to the voice.*

They turned, and off they ran, into the unknown, vanishing right in front of me.

In that split second, I had to decide whether to stay with John or follow the kids into the black hole. I knew what John would tell me to do: *Go after the kids.*

I was soon past a ditch and up on a side road with a young couple who'd seen the crash and were standing by their car, directing people toward them. It was the first moment I saw my kids after sending them fleeing from the carnage.

As the smoke billowed up and out from the accident, we scrambled into the couple's car. But as I peered out, my heart sank. John wasn't with us, and I couldn't see him anywhere.

"John!" I screamed his name until finally Reese pointed past me.

"There he is! There's Dad!" she said.

He hurried across the ditch and up the small embankment toward us, carrying some of our belongings, his phone, his wallet. That was John, Mr. Practical, hoping to save what he could before the car was engulfed in fire.

With a shaky voice I tried to describe to a 9-1-1 operator where we were. Calm was out the window by now. I was yelling at, more than talking to, the dispatcher, trying to convey our location, what happened, begging her to send multiple ambulances. It was all a blur as I watched the hot fire grow larger and larger through the still-choking dust storm.

Before long, ambulances, fire trucks, and bystanders were gathering around the scene.

While the kids sat in the back of an ambulance, entertained by some emergency personnel, a truck driver ran up the embankment, leaned over, and threw up. He'd tried to save the driver who'd hit the first truck but wasn't able to do so. The man had died on impact.

Five semis altogether were involved, along with our SUV. Yet here we stood, all of us, surviving without even a scratch. All because John had an "urgent hunch" that we weren't safe where we were.

But in the middle of all this chaos, something else was happening, something that no one else could see but me: I began seeing something very specific, in my mind's eye: *Jeremiah 29:11*. And it wouldn't leave me. Over and over, like a pesky sibling tapping my shoulder, it kept flashing through my mind...*Jeremiah 29:11*.

When we were finally driven away from the accident site and into Groom, Texas, we passed one of the largest crosses in the country. I peered up at it as we drove by.

Jeremiah 29:11.

I didn't have a clue what that meant, except I knew it was in the Bible.

To be honest, it was getting annoying. We were in the middle of so much commotion, trying to move our luggage, find a motel, get settled, call the insurance, and call Kirk to tell him what happened. I was suffocating under the circumstances.

But this verse would not leave me alone.

The only place available for us to go was a tiny family-run motel, ages old, and definitely not my cup of tea. But we were without a car, without belongings, hungry, and exhausted physically and emotionally.

Still, in the forefront of my mind, it continued: *Jeremiah 29:11.*

As soon as we got to our room, I burst through the door and ran straight to the nightstand. I knew one thing for certain: In almost every hotel or motel across the country, there is a Gideon Bible.

And sure enough, there it was.

I flipped through the pages until I found it—Jeremiah 29:11.

I put my finger to the words and read it carefully in the King James Version. I would later know it better by the NIV: "'For I know the plans I have for you,' declares the Lord. 'Plans to prosper you and not harm you, plans to give you a hope and a future.'"

I sat there on the bed, Bible open in my lap, realizing God was speaking to me. Loudly, but in the softest of ways. In the middle of chaos, He chose to whisper to me.

This is what the Lord wanted me to know. Through every step I'd taken, through every perceived failure, He had a plan. He had a purpose.

I had not been overlooked.

Not for a single day.

I broke down on the floor and wept. He spoke so clearly to me:

Bridgette, I've never forgotten you. All those years that you sat back and watched...all those years that you were hurt and frustrated and disappointed...all those times you heard, "not today"...now I will show you all the wonderful things I have planned for you and your family. In My timing, I saved all of you today because I have a plan and a purpose for your life, but you need to trust Me.

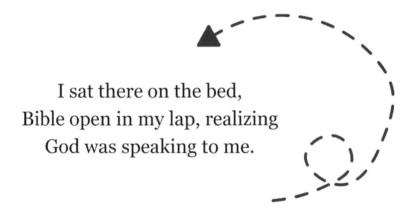

I sat there on the bed, Bible open in my lap, realizing God was speaking to me.

The accident had shaken me. Then God came dramatically into it all and spoke over my life. All I wanted in this moment was to go home with my family and just allow ourselves to weep and hold each other safely. Even though we had escaped unscathed, my mind raced with all the "what if's" despite my best effort to keep it from going there.

John was having his own journey in all of this, processing many things. We no longer had a car and barely had suitcases. What were we supposed to do? We were stuck in a small motel in Groom, Texas, dealing with the aftershock of a near-death experience. How would we even get home if we wanted to?

"I don't have a plan," John said, then added emphatically,

"but I know we're not going to let Satan win. We're not going home. If we go home right now, all of us are just going to run this scene over and over in our heads."

He was right. He knew me well. He knew all of us well.

The following minutes, hours, and days were all filled with their own beautiful miracles, or "God-winks" as I call them. A Christian tow truck driver offered to get us to Amarillo, Texas, the only place that had hotels and restaurants and car rental companies. That gentleman blessed us with his generous and empathetic spirit.

We arrived at the emergency room in Amarillo to be assessed for our injuries. Everyone there already knew who we were and had been expecting our arrival. They were so gracious. The doctor, recognizing we'd been displaced and had lost everything in the crash, offered us his home to stay in. An Uber driver drove us around for free to get supplies we needed. The hotel paid for our stay. God poured out so many blessings on us!

Then an incredibly generous couple we knew rented us a limousine that drove us four hours to the Dallas airport, where they bought us tickets to fly to Nashville and stay at the hotel where the K-LOVE Awards were being hosted.

That's right. Despite the horror of this accident, we somehow, by the grace of God, still made it to Nashville. We saw Kirk and Chelsea and we all hugged a little tighter, a little longer.

It could not have had a better or more beautiful ending.

But as it turned out, my journey, at least with God, was just beginning.

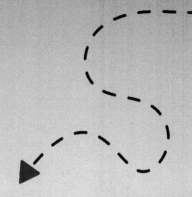

CHAPTER 9
THE PROMISE AND THE BLESSING

BEFORE WE WERE SHUTTLED out of Groom to Amarillo by God's grace and the tow truck driver He sent named Al, we learned from the surviving truck drivers what exactly had gone wrong.

The rule on the road, for truckers anyway, is to never, ever stop. Even if you can't see where you're going, even if you have to slow down considerably, don't stop your truck. When you can't see what's ahead of you, trust the rule of the road, otherwise what's behind you may catch up in a destructive way. Unfortunately, someone had stopped.

As I considered my life, I realized it paralleled that rule. Despite all the rejection, I had never stopped. Ever. Sure, I had grown up in the middle of a full house of growing pains, and I had my fears and disappointments. The agent hadn't chosen me. The choreographer hadn't chosen me. But God had. The Bible says that He chose me before the foundation of the world.

After the accident, I started thinking about all the promises in the Bible that God gave me, verses like:

"For I know the plans I have for you," declares the Lord, "plans to prosper you and not to harm you, plans to give you hope and a future." – Jeremiah 29:11

The Lord will keep you from all harm—he will watch over your life; the Lord will watch over your coming and going both now and forevermore. – Psalm 121:7-8

As I considered all the blessings God had given me, I started to look at my life differently. For instance, when my son Cameron was going to middle school, things for him suddenly spiraled. His grades began failing. The class sizes were so big he couldn't keep up. I quickly realized public school was not for him. I told John that if we didn't do something quickly, we were going to lose our son.

We pulled Cameron out and put him in a private school. We had to sacrifice a lot to afford private school for him, but we did, and Cameron attended from seventh grade all the way through high school.

I'll never forget the day of his graduation when he walked across that stage and received his high school diploma. There were times when I didn't know if that day would ever come, but there he was, hat high on his head and diploma in hand. He had done so well in private school. He was on the honor roll and the soccer team.

During a special moment in the graduation ceremony, a video played that the seniors had made for their parents. As the parents watched the video, each of the seniors came down and handed them a rose. Cameron hugged me and said, "Mom, thank you. Thank you for sacrificing everything you did to get me to graduate. If it weren't for you and Dad, I wouldn't be here. I wouldn't be standing here with my diploma. So, thank you."

Soon after, he went to York, England, for a year and played for a soccer academy. It was so beautiful to see him continue to thrive and pursue his dreams.

During another year, at Christmas, Cameron offered to take us to lunch. When we came back, John and I walked into our kitchen. There was a brand-new, stainless steel refrigerator with a bow on it. Everett turned to John and me and said, "Merry Christmas!"

"Everett, this is from you?" I asked. He was only 18!

"Yeah. I know you and Dad want to start redoing the interior of the house, and I'm hoping that this new refrigerator will kind of get you started."

I was stunned! Everett had begun a brand-new job a year prior as a coffee barista at Dutch Bros Coffee. We all thought it was funny because Everett doesn't drink coffee. He'd never made a coffee drink before in his life, but he picked it up quickly and worked incredibly hard. I remembered him working overtime, all shifts, not realizing what he was saving for. Seeing the stainless steel refrigerator in our kitchen from him was a blessing I can barely describe. Beyond the "gift," it was his generous heart that made my own heart burst with joy.

"Everett," I said, "this must have wiped out your bank account."

"It did," he replied. "But Mom, I know you and Dad have been working really hard to get started on the kitchen, and I just wanted to help you guys out. And don't worry about my bank account. I can just work hard to get it back up again."

While considering these moments, one day it hit me—if I had been pursuing my dreams of being a performer and traveling, I might have missed all these important moments and many more. All the daily details. All the most treasured elements of motherhood. I would not have been home to build these bonds with my kids.

Maybe God's plan for my life was better than my own. I also realized God did give me gifts along the way. He gave me many opportunities to use my gifts in a way that didn't compromise all the other gifts and blessings He had for my life. I had a joyous 25-year career of being a stand-in, in Hollywood.

As if that weren't enough, one year Kirk came to me and said, "Hey Bridgette, I'm doing a Christmas movie, and there's a part in the movie that is my character's sister. I wanted to know if you wanted to play my sister in the movie."

"Of course!" That was the year I filmed *Saving Christmas* with him. I was on a set and in hair and makeup and wardrobe. I wasn't a stand-in this time. I was one of the *co-stars...*on the *big screen!*

I was in the grocery store one day, and a little old couple saw me and said, "You're that lady from the movie, *Saving Christmas!*"

"Yeah, I am!" What an amazing time. It was one of my most memorable and fun opportunities.

Soon after, I decided to take my first ballroom dance class. Through all my years of dancing, I had experimented with many styles, but never done ballroom. I didn't realize that Latin was part of ballroom dancing. I always thought ballroom was what I had seen on TV with the waltz and the foxtrot and smooth dances.

During my very first ballroom dance class, the instructor tried to teach me the waltz, rumba, and foxtrot. He kept saying, "Bridgette, you must stop moving your hips so much."

"I can't help it. It's just natural."

"We're going to start learning some Latin then."

That's where I began learning the cha-cha, the salsa, the samba, and more Latin dances. After we were done with my very first class, he pulled me aside and said, "Bridgette, you're very good and I want you to compete in a ballroom dance competition in three months."

I thought he was crazy. "There's no way," I breathed.

"I really think you can do it."

I was shocked. I couldn't help but remember a certain audition for which I'd so highly qualified. That door had slammed shut. Now here I was, underqualified in my mind, being told I was ready enough to compete in a ballroom competition!

I smiled. God certainly has His own way of doing things, and His own way of handing out blessings in His perfect timing.

For four months I trained in a dance studio and learned the Latin dances. I competed in my very first dance competition here in Palm Springs, the 2018 Desert Classic Ballroom Championship, and had a blast! I competed in twelve heats and placed first through third in every single heat.

It was one of the most fun and memorable experiences ever.

Then it began to sink in…

By God saying no and closing all those doors, He was taking care of me all along. I had been wanting God to fulfill *my* plans rather than considering what *His* plans for my life were. It was becoming clearer each day—God's story for us is always better than our own.

Now I see my life differently. I see it through the promises of God. I'm excited and ready for the next chapter of my story. God continues to remind me that the most important part of my story isn't what didn't happen. <u>It's what's happening right now</u>. This is His story. He is the author—it's constant, it's ongoing, it's active. I don't want to miss a single moment of it by looking back with regret or stopping in my tracks due to fear or discouragement.

My story is all part of His bigger story. It just so happens that the greatest adventures of our lives come into focus when we embrace His plans.

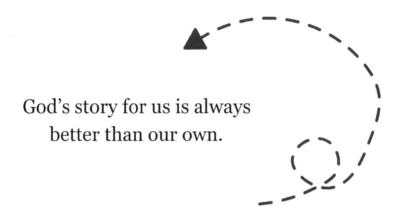

God's story for us is always better than our own.

Maybe you have had a season of feeling overlooked. Or maybe you are in that season right now. Maybe you are feeling sad and unnoticed, unrecognized, and unfulfilled. Maybe you're angry with God and asking Him, "Why?" Maybe you're going through a season in your life with your spouse or a child or a friend, and you want to give up. Perhaps you have an overwhelming sense of emptiness, wondering if God hears your cries and sees your tears.

God sees everything, hears everything, and knows your heart before you do. He knows your suffering, your longing, and it's only through Jesus that any of us can feel whole again.

Let me encourage you to hold on. Don't give up. God has a plan and a purpose for everything in your life. Remind yourself of God's promises for your life every single day so you can see things clearly and differently. There are people in this world who have everything that anyone could ever want. Fame, celebrity, status, wealth, influence. Most of them are very sad and empty people. My siblings are an exception to this rule only because their hope and fulfillment come from God's promises, not their accomplishments or opportunities. *That* is what makes all the difference.

I have met and worked with so many of these unfulfilled people. They're sad and empty because they've lost their real purpose in life. Our purpose as human beings is to live in the will of God. For some, that means motherhood. For others, it's being a devoted spouse. For others, it is to provide for their families or to raise the next generation or to help those who are in need. For all of us, though, our most important purpose is to point people to Jesus.

God never forgets about us or our dreams. He wants you to trust Him with them. Can you do that? Will you trust that? Far from being overlooked, you've been chosen by an almighty and powerful God to be His child and do His will, to be blessed abundantly in the currency of heaven, which does not tarnish nor spoil.

God sees you and He never takes His eyes off you. He is the most trustworthy of all.

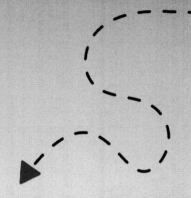

EPILOGUE

IF YOU'VE MADE it this far, I thank you for taking this journey with me...this little look into my life, a life I wouldn't trade for the world. It's who I am, and it's the life that built me. Each memory has a place and a purpose in my life, the good and the bad. I remember my brother telling me that his pastor told him one time how we don't find God. God isn't lost. God finds us. If you've picked up this book today, I believe that's a God-wink. God is finding you right this very moment.

Maybe you've known Jesus for a long time, but maybe it's time to come back to Him and trust Him again. Maybe for some of you, it's the first time you're exploring what it means to have a relationship with God. That's great to hear. After all, your Creator is, together with you, writing the story of your life. It makes good sense to be friends, not enemies, with the Author, cultivating a hopeful and humble heart.

You can talk to Him like you would an intimate friend. Thank Him for His faithfulness and kindness towards you.

Trust Him with all your heart. Turn from evil, and He will direct your path.

Let's pray together.

> *God, I need You. I need You to come into my life just as I am. I give my heart to You completely. Lord, I want to change my ways. I want to follow You. And Lord, I may not know how to do that entirely, but I trust You will guide me. I ask that You forgive me of my sins and that You cleanse me from the inside out. I want to be a follower of Jesus Christ and have a personal relationship with You. Thank You for sending Your Son to earth to bear punishment for my sins and raising Him from the dead so that I may have new life within Him.*
>
> *Lord, I ask that You lead me to people who will help me, guide me, and build me up. I want to learn more about You. Allow me to be a light to those who need You. Use me in ways that I never thought I could be useful in spreading the Good News of Your love and grace.*
>
> *Lord, I know that there are going to be challenges, but I am ready to follow You. Draw me close every single day. Give me the desire to read Your Word, understand it, and apply it. Protect me from danger. Forgive my sins. Forgive me for not trusting You. Turn me away from the things that are putting a barrier between us and bring my heart closer to Yours every day.*
>
> *Amen.*

God's word tells us that, "If you confess with your mouth, 'Jesus is Lord,' and believe in your heart that God raised Him from the dead, you will be saved." (Romans 10:9). You can come to Him in your brokenness, your anger, your suffering, your loneliness. God will never turn away from you. If you seek Him with all your heart, in humility, with a willingness to divorce yourself from your past and current sins, He will lead you into greater, more meaningful things than you could have ever imagined. Will you turn to Him today? If so, then I encourage you to read the Bible and follow what you read. God will never let you down. Join a local Bible-teaching church and find a group of loving and courageous believers you can grow with. I promise, you'll be glad you did.

Blessings,

For further reading:
John 3:16-17
Romans 6:23
2 Corinthians 5:17

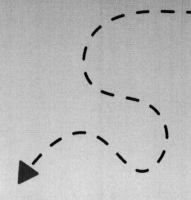

DISCUSSION QUESTIONS

1. Bridgette describes a happy childhood where she was just beginning to understand some gifts she was born with. What were some talents or gifts that you first discovered in your childhood? Did discovering these gifts shape any of your dreams for your life as you grew older? If so, how?

2. What do you remember as being the first big disappointment in your life? How do you think it affected you as a child? What about as an adult?

3. Bridgette describes herself as an optimist. Do you think you are an optimist or a pessimist? What do you think are the strengths and weaknesses of each personality type?

4. When others around you have success, are you prone to cheer them on or is that a hard thing for you to do? Who in your life has been a good cheerleader for you, able to cheer you on without needing their own success? What kind of mindset shift helps you cheer

people on when you're not enjoying your own success?

5. Bridgette describes how a painful stretch in her family's life began a journey of faith for the family. Have you had a similar experience when a painful time has led you toward God? Why do you think we are more prone to hear God's voice during those times?

6. As Bridgette began her own faith journey, God showed her how important a godly relationship was in marriage, and she made the commitment to look for someone who met those standards. If faith has come into your life, what was one of the first things God asked you to begin considering in your walk of faith?

7. Bridgette describes her belief that the *Wizard of Oz* opportunity was finally all her dreams coming true, only to discover that wasn't God's plan at all. Name a time that you believed God was doing something big in your life, and it turned out not to be the case. What were the feelings you had to manage your way through? Do those still linger to this day?

8. As Bridgette moved on in life without her dreams coming true, God slowly began to speak to her through small and big moments over several years, beckoning her into a closer relationship with Him. Discuss some ways God has been calling you into a deeper relationship with Him.

9. Discuss with the group ways you have felt God has overlooked you in life. Spend some time praying with your group about this and asking God to show you

how He has not overlooked you in life. Continue to work through this through journaling and praying over the next few weeks.

10. Spend time this week reading the book of *Ruth* in the Bible and the story of Ruth and Naomi. Write out some thoughts on how we often feel overlooked but how God has a plan and purpose for redeeming us all.

11. Spend some time alone and write God a letter. Share with Him your thoughts and feelings. Tell Him what's on your heart and ask Him to speak to you. If you've asked Jesus into your heart for the first time, ask Him for His guidance and to lead you to next steps.

ACKNOWLEDGMENTS

John - You have been my biggest support, encouragement, and the best husband I ever could have asked and prayed for. Thank you for always believing in me (even when we first met). I'll love you always.

Cameron, Everett & Reese - Thank you for pushing me to do this project. On days that were hard you kept telling me "you can!" I love you all and I'm so Blessed to call you mine.

Kirk, Melissa & Candace - Who would have thought I would be writing a book about our crazy adventures as kids? Thank you for your encouragement, your willingness to help me and the deepest love I receive from you all is nothing but a treasure.

Mom & Dad - I did it! I wrote my first book, and see, it wasn't a Cameron "Tell All!" I thank you both for your love and continued support in all things BIG or small. I love you.

Chelsea & Olivia - Being my second and third set of eyes on this project has been such a Blessing and the truthfulness of your words means so much to me. I love you both so much.

Rene - I'm so glad that you said YES to this project. The laughter and tears have been so much fun and I'm so thankful for your friendship.

Fred & Michael - Thank you for your kindness and your giving hearts to make this book possible.

Home Group - What a Blessing it is to do life with you! Each week we grow more and more as individuals through God's word and great food! You all bring such joy to my heart. Thank you all for your prayers, encouragement and help with this project. #raptureready

And finally to ALL my dearest girlfriends - Whether I've known you for years or we have just become friends (you know who you are), you make life more fun. You make me laugh. You make me cry. You've prayed with me, for me, and over me, and I can't tell you what a special place you have in my heart. I'm Blessed to call you my friend.

Bridgette Cameron

If you're a child of the 80's, you might have seen the siblings of **Bridgette Cameron Ridenour** grace the cover of every *Bop, Teen Beat,* or *Tiger Beat* magazine on store shelves. Or maybe – just maybe – they were even on your own bedroom walls.

The sister to Kirk Cameron and Candace Cameron Bure, Bridgette is now stepping into her own speaking career along with launching "Overlooked." A terrifying, but life-changing, moment with her family brought her closer to them, to God, and ultimately to her purpose. Bridgette's testimony of finding purpose through her life verse, Jeremiah 29:11, is a message of inexhaustible hope, fulfillment, a deeper joy, and an understanding that God's timing is perfect...and His plans for us are far better than our own.

Bridgette is currently speaking at women's events and conferences across the United States in hopes of encouraging and inspiring anyone who has ever felt overlooked or unsure of their future. God has a plan, a purpose, and a promise for each of us! And His divine vision is so much brighter than ours ever could be on our own.

Bridgette currently lives in Palm Springs, California with her husband John, (children) Cameron, Everett, and Reese – and sweet Goldendoodle Nova.

Contact Bridgette for booking information at
BridgetteCameron.com

Umbrella Ministries

A Support Ministry Reaching Out to the Hurts and Hearts of Mothers Who Have Experienced the Loss of a Child.

Every day there are thousands of mothers who have lost a child, living in the depths of despair, feeling they have lost all hope.

We offer support to bereaved mothers by:

- Opportunities to share and talk about the loss if their child through support groups led by mothers who have also lost a child. To see if a support group is in your area go to RESOURCES on the website.

- Providing articles of support and encouragement filled with hope and comfort. Moms can sign up through the website for weekly devotions and quarterly newsletters.

- Annual "Journey of the Heart" retreats and conferences throughout the United States with speakers and workshops designed for mothers who have experienced the loss of a child.

Find more information at UmbrellaMinistries.org

In Memoriam

To my beautiful daughter Sofia.

To hold you, only for a moment,
was one of the most beautiful moments with you.

I love you beyond words. I miss you and I can't wait to see you again.

◀-- -- ⌣ -- -▶

Sofia Ridenour
08.08.05

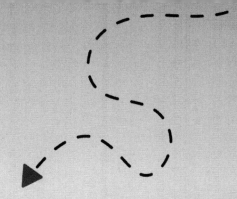

JOURNAL PAGES
